The Study Skills
Handbook

The Study Skills
Handbook

More than 75 Strategies for Better Learning

by Judith Dodge

SCHOLASTIC
PROFESSIONAL BOOKS

New York • Toronto • London • Auckland • Sydney

To Arnie, my husband and best friend
and to my wonderful children,
Michael and Gregory.

Design by Drew Hires
Cover and Interior Illustrations by Drew Hires
Cover Design by Vincent Ceci

ISBN 0-590-49510-0

12 11 10 9 8 7 6 5 4 3 2 1   1 2 3 4 5/9
Printed in the U.S.A.

Acknowledgments

Thanks to:

All the teachers I have worked with over the years who explored with me the many ways to improve student learning through better study skills instruction. Their professional knowledge, experience, advice and feedback were invaluable.

Esther Fusco, Ph.D., my friend and colleague, who encouraged me to follow my instincts in developing a comprehensive program to integrate study skills into the curriculum and "nurtured the seed" which led to my concentration on programs and materials, including staff development, parent education and modeling lessons, to help students "learn how to learn."

The teachers at the Babylon Grade School who tried out many of my strategies, refined them and created their own to make learning and studying more meaningful for their students. The systematic approach to study skills instruction that we developed over the last few years was the end result of their hard work, time and effort.

Diane Abrams, Rita Bartenback, Barbara Campasano, Patricia Dalpiaz and Luise Lutz, of the Babylon School District, for their eagerness to share ideas and create new ones as we co-authored *Study Survival Guide*, and Suzanne DeMottie for naming my "Flashy Review" strategy.

Carol Crowley, my son Gregory's first grade teacher in the Port Jefferson School District, who reminded me all about the importance of completing "must-do's before enjoying "want-to-do's."

Linda Hirschenfeld of the Port Jefferson Library who gladly helped me each time I called on her as I researched material for this book.

Donna Levinson whose "Ticket to the Test" reinforced my own ideas for helping students to engage in "active" study strategies at home. A special thanks for all the wisdom she shared with my husband and me when our son, Michael, was fortunate enough to have her as his teacher in fifth grade, especially in helping me to better understand the role of parents in helping children succeed in school.

Donna Levinson and Ellen Diamond's sixth grade students in the Port Jefferson School District, who eagerly shared with me examples of their own creative study strategies.

Dolores Belzarano, Fran DiPiazza and Bob Simione's fifth grade students in the Comsewogue School District who tested out my study strategies and were overheard saying, "this isn't like work; this studying is more like fun."

My husband, Arnie, who helped me edit my first drafts and willingly picked up the pieces at home when I was under the pressure of my final deadlines. His loving support has always given me strength and hope; my son, Michael, whose brilliant computer skills saved many a lost document; and my son, Gregory, who tried his best to be patient and quiet while Mommy was busy writing her book.

My editors at Scholastic: Terry Cooper, who first recognized the "updated look" of my materials and encouraged me to put my ideas together for this book; and Virginia Dooley, whose wise suggestions helped clarify many portions of this book and who gently encouraged me to consider changes to make this book better.

Table of Contents

Introduction

I had been teaching for ten years when I came to the realization that few of my students had any idea of what it meant to "study." Overly concerned with content, I had not paid enough attention to the *process* of learning. And my students were struggling because of it. I decided to redefine my role as an educator and launch a campaign to help students learn "how to learn." For the next few years, I researched the topics of learning strategies and study skills—those learned abilities which enable students to systematically *plan, access, record, organize, encode* and *use* information on their own. I came to believe that integrating study skills into content curriculum would have a synergistic effect upon learning.

This book is the result of the experimentation, research, writing and invention of hundreds of people. I have worked with all of these strategies, refining ideas about them, collaborating on new designs and introducing them to thousands of teachers, parents and students. I have seen them make a difference in the kids who use them and the teachers who take the time to integrate them into their lessons.

The strategies I suggest are easy to incorporate in already established curricula. Rather than a lock-step approach to study skills, this book makes it easy for you as teachers to choose from dozens of strategies to find the ones that best suit the needs and learning styles of your students.

Why should students learn study skills? Study skills empower students to manage the demands of school. Armed with study tools and strategies, more students are able to succeed in school. Instead of waiting for the natural trial-and-error process of "learning how to learn" to take place, we can intervene earlier and eliminate the frustration for both teachers and students engaged in this struggle. And because study skills are learned *abilities*, all students can be taught to use them, not just those who would eventually learn them on their own. We cannot teach students all the facts they need to know; we must provide them, instead, with some of the strategies they will need as they continue in the lifelong process of learning.

When should students learn study skills? When students enter school, we should begin to lay the foundation for these skills. The structure we provide in school and the support we enlist from home set the stage for future success. Instruction in study skills should continue throughout the grades. Each year, the subsequent teacher should build upon past experience and provide repeated opportunities for practice with increasingly more sophisticated materials. In the early grades, most of the instruction is teacher directed; in the middle grades, students practice study skills using a variety of strategies to accommodate different learning styles; in the upper grades, students have an opportunity to choose the strategies that work best for them and apply them in independent learning situations.

Where should students learn study skills? These skills should be incorporated into every classroom and every subject area. There is a synergistic effect upon learning when content material is taught along with study skills. Taught in isolation, study skills are rarely used by students in other classes. Students need content-specific applications of the various strategies; they need to see that study skills apply to all of their learning.

Who should teach study skills to students? Every teacher at every grade level should be involved. As teachers, we should share the responsibility for helping students to become independent, self-directed learners by helping students develop strong skills through repeated practice.

What about parents? Should they be involved in the process? Absolutely. Parents can support good teaching efforts. They can certainly provide a home environment that maximizes the likelihood of studying and learning. Their best efforts to show their children how to study, however, can't compare to those of a teacher who models and integrates study skills into his or her lessons and holds students accountable for using the strategies. Many parents are not at home to structure homework and study time so, for many students, the only chance for success will come from the efforts of the school.

Which study skills should be taught? I've organized Chapters 1-9 of this book around important study skill areas. All of the skills cannot be addressed in one or two years. Ideally, a school district should provide staff development and allow teachers to develop a suggested scope and sequence for grades K-12, where responsibility for instruction is shared among all grade levels. If, however, you have decided to teach study skills on your own, identify four or five of the skills you consider the most important and integrate them throughout your content curriculum. Even in one year, you will see an improvement in the ability of your students to direct their own learning. Try to work together with one or two other teachers; the additional reinforcement will have an even greater impact on student learning!

How should study skills be taught? Students will benefit from a unified and systematic approach to study skills instruction. If teachers agree on the goals of a good study skills program and make study skills instruction an integral part the curriculum across the grades, more students will learn "how to learn."

Consideration must be given to the various learning styles of students. No one method will meet the needs of all students. Reciting during study time may be the best strategy for an auditory learner, but a visual learner may learn best by making a chart or creating a Venn diagram. The best way to teach study skills is to offer a repertoire of strategies and help students determine which methods work best for each of them.

Good study behaviors must be modeled and students must be given frequent opportunities to use them. Provide many opportunities for additional trial and error, feedback and correction. Expect to model the same skill many times; remember that mastery of some concepts or skills requires hundreds—even thousands—of attempts.

Here are some final thoughts before we discuss how to implement various strategies. As you increase the study skills component in your curriculum, consider yourself successful if you:

✔ **raise student awareness of what studying and learning entail**
✔ **teach students to make positive choices with respect to their schooling**
✔ **help students retain more through "active" study strategies**
✔ **increase student ownership of their progress in school**
✔ **see evidence of student use of study strategies**
✔ **hear even one student proclaim that studying this way is more fun!**

The strategies I have chosen to share with you have a common thread. They all are designed to lead to greater independence on the part of students. Although, at the middle grades the activities will require much teacher modeling and classroom instruction, ultimately these skills will transfer to more independent use on the part of students.

A Note About Using This Book

The title and page number of the reproducibles suggested for each chapter are listed in the Advance Preparation section. Any time a reproducible is mentioned, its title is printed in boldface.

Chapter 1

Organizational Skills

Starting the Process

Background

Students who are disorganized often waste a great deal of time looking for misplaced assignments and materials and settling down to work. Since organizational skills are crucial to a child's feeling of being in control of his or her schoolwork, work on developing these skills should begin early in the year. Then students should be given multiple opportunities to practice new behaviors for organizing themselves. They must be convinced that their new habits will make schoolwork easier and, therefore, be worth spending time on.

The focus of this chapter will be on helping students develop useful ways of recording assignments, keeping track of all paperwork and requirements and maintaining organized notebooks.

Advance Preparation

Over the summer or on the first day of school, send home a list of required materials. In addition to your usual list, be sure to request that students bring in one plastic, two-pocket folder, five folders and some zip-top plastic bags. The longer lasting plastic folder will be used as a Travel Folder, the additional folders will be used to file papers and the zip-top bags will be used to store sets of flashcards.

Decide whether your students will be using a particular assignment book for the year or an assignment sheet such as the **Homework Log** (see page 17) which you will distribute weekly. Be sure to have the books or sheets available on the first day of school. Also have on hand copies of the following reproducibles:

✔ **Phone Friends** (*page 18*)
✔ **At School Checklist** (*page 19*)
✔ **At Home Checklist** (*page 19*)
✔ **My Reminder Checklist** (*page 19*)

Strategies

Homework Log

Distribute a copy of the **Homework Log** each week if you choose not to use a commercial assignment book. Note that there is room to record the assignments and a box to check off after each assignment is completed. In addition, there is a place to list other things your students will be required to remember, such as signed permission slips, money for lunch, sneakers for gym. There is a box for recording upcoming tests, projects and assignments. Finally, there is a place to write a goal for the week and room for a parent's signature.

Check that students are recording their assignments completely. Notify parents if their signatures are to be required. You can use this Homework Log as a means to communicate with all parents or just with parents of students who need additional structure.

Phone Friends

Phone Friends is a list of classmates' telephone numbers. Each student chooses two friends in each of his or her classes and records their phone numbers. Remind students that homework is *their* responsibility and encourage them to call a friend when they are absent or unsure about an assignment.

Travel Folder

A Travel Folder allows the student to keep daily assignments and papers organized. One side of a two-pocket, plastic folder is labeled "To Do" and includes any loose worksheets for homework, notices to go home, tests or permission slips to be signed and the Homework Log or assignment book. By keeping track of homework this way, the student needs to look in only one place at the end of the day to see which texts, notebooks and other materials need to go home. The second pocket is labeled "Done" or "Completed." It holds any completed assignments, signed papers or messages that must be returned to school.

Reminder Checklists

To help students develop organizational skills, help them create checklists to remind them of their responsibilities. An **At School Checklist** can be kept on their desk or in their locker. It will remind them to check their assignment sheet and bring home any required material and projects.

The **At Home Checklist** will remind them to pack all homework, texts and other materials for school. It may also list any chores that need to be done and include a reminder to eat a good breakfast before leaving for school. A blank checklist, **My Reminder Checklist**, is included so students can make their own lists.

Locker Logic

Students who use lockers often have a great deal of trouble keeping them organized and finding what they need in them. You might suggest that students keep A.M. books on the top and P.M. books on the bottom of their lockers. Show them how to color-code their notebooks and texts by drawing a thick magic marker line around their subject notebook in the same color as the corresponding textbook cover. Suggest a locker checklist to record which books need to be brought home. (Students using a Travel Folder which includes an assignment record would probably not need this checklist.) Schedule periodic clean-outs because no system is foolproof, and students will have to reorganize themselves periodically.

Homework Habits

Just as we try to post homework in the same spot on the board each day and we have students put completed homework in a particular place each morning, it's a good idea for students to place their bookbags or backpacks in the same spot each day when they get home. This eliminates wasting time later when they are looking for homework materials. The habit of placing things in one spot should extend to students placing completed assignments immediately in their Travel Folders, and then in their bookbag or backpack for return to school the next day. Suggest they study in the same place each day, with necessary supplies at hand in a box or drawer. This will lead to an easier transition from play to study time. Encourage parents to establish a set time for children to begin homework. You might send a note home explaining how the establishment of routines allows habits to develop and homework to become less of a source of conflict.

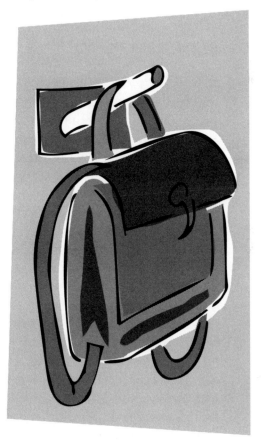

Notebook Know-How

Teachers who engage in strategies to improve notebook organization acknowledge that the benefits make it worth the time and effort. Their students learn important lessons about maintaining notebooks that are useful for independent study.

At the beginning of the year, give students a handout that outlines the specific format that you would like their notebooks to follow. Include directions for labeling each of the sections and dating each entry. Some teachers choose to be quite specific by having students label all first semester entries 1-1, 1-2, 1-3 and so on, all second semester entries 2-1, 2-2, 2-3 and so on. In this way, students can easily identify any missing entries by checking a master list which is posted in the room. Tell students that you'll be looking at notebooks on a regular basis, perhaps three to four times a year. Don't try to check all of the notebooks at the same time; instead, choose five or ten to review at once. Using a simple checklist, you can rapidly accomplish the task.

Daily Entry

Another strategy for encouraging better notebook organization is the daily entry. Each day ask students to solve a review math problem, write a new vocabulary word and definition, copy a stanza of a poem or record any other information relevant to a topic you are studying in class. Students should label and date each entry. After two weeks of this activity, give a surprise notebook "test" that asks students to find, for instance, the day they copied a particular word and its definition, or what the solution was to the math problem on a certain date. Many students find that this "easy A" (or some other reward) motivates them to continue keeping their notebooks organized and accurate. After a while, doing so becomes a habit.

Open-Notebook Tests

Finally, improve notebook organization by giving open-notebook tests. Tell students ahead of time that you will allow them to use their notebooks from time to time on a test. While open-notebook tests may provide students some easy answers, they also encourage more accurate and complete note taking. Since good notes are critical to good studying, it is worth the occasional trade-off.

Teaching Suggestions and Extension Ideas

1. Checklists tend to be useful for a while and then seem to lose their effectiveness. Plan to have students use them for a few weeks at a time, and then put them aside. When the need to refocus on organizational skills arises, pull them out again. Explain to parents how they might use them in the same way.

2. For a child living in two homes because of a divorce or custodial situation, the problem of organization can be even greater. In this case, it would be most helpful to send a note to parents in both homes about how best to keep their child on top of schoolwork. (Check the legality of this with your principal first.) You might include suggestions for a quiet study area with school materials in a box or drawer in each home. Send them copies of the **Reminder Checklists** so that the child can be sure to leave each home with everything that he or she needs for school.

Homewok Log   *Week of* _____

MONDAY

☐ MATH _____	☐ SOCIAL STUDIES _____
☐ SCIENCE _____	☐ OTHER _____
☐ ENGLISH/LANGUAGE ARTS _____	☐ REMINDERS _____

TUESDAY

☐ MATH _____	☐ SOCIAL STUDIES _____
☐ SCIENCE _____	☐ OTHER _____
☐ ENGLISH/LANGUAGE ARTS _____	☐ REMINDERS _____

WEDNESDAY

☐ MATH _____	☐ SOCIAL STUDIES _____
☐ SCIENCE _____	☐ OTHER _____
☐ ENGLISH/LANGUAGE ARTS _____	☐ REMINDERS _____

THURSDAY

☐ MATH _____	☐ SOCIAL STUDIES _____
☐ SCIENCE _____	☐ OTHER _____
☐ ENGLISH/LANGUAGE ARTS _____	☐ REMINDERS _____

FRIDAY

☐ MATH _____	☐ SOCIAL STUDIES _____
☐ SCIENCE _____	☐ OTHER _____
☐ ENGLISH/LANGUAGE ARTS _____	☐ REMINDERS _____

UPCOMING TESTS/PROJECTS/ASSIGNMENTS	MY GOAL FOR THIS WEEK IS:

Parent's Signature _____

Phone Friends

On this page record the telephone numbers of two friends in each of your classes. In case you are absent or are unsure of an assignment, you will be able to call someone to help you out.

English/Language Arts

_____ | _____
_____ | _____

Social Studies

_____ | _____
_____ | _____

Math

_____ | _____
_____ | _____

Science

_____ | _____
_____ | _____

Other:_____

_____ | _____
_____ | _____

Other:_____

_____ | _____
_____ | _____

POST THIS LIST OF PHONE NUMBERS **AT HOME** WHERE YOU STUDY

Reminder Checklists

At Home

❑ Pack all homework, texts, notebooks in bookbag or backpack.

❑ Bring lunch or lunch money.

❑ Place any signed papers in Travel Folder.

❑ Things that need to be done before school:_____

_____

_____

❑ Eat a good breakfast.

At School

❑ Before packing to leave, check homework assignment sheet.

❑ Bring home any texts, notebooks or other materials that you will need.

❑ Ask teacher about any upcoming tests or projects (when it is due, what it covers and so on).

❑ Place in Travel Folder any notices handed out to go home.

My Reminder Checklist

❑ _____

❑ _____

❑ _____

❑ _____

❑ _____

Chapter 2

"Active" Study Strategies

Learning By Doing

Background

Many teachers carefully plan a multisensory approach to their lessons in order to increase student learning. For example, in a Social Studies class, students might *read* about the Europeans' interest in finding an all-water route to Asia during the 1400s; they might *write* a list of the discoveries of Spanish, French and Portuguese explorers; they might *discuss* the French and Spanish influence on the culture of the United States; they might *draw* a map showing the routes the European explorers took. They might come dressed up and *simulate* an explorer's court presentation to Queen Isabella and King Ferdinand requesting money for a voyage. Few of those students, however, use multisensory strategies when studying on their own. If we ask students how they study, most will reply that they "look over notes and reread the text." They will quickly add that they soon find themselves daydreaming or falling asleep; their senses are not engaged.

It is not enough to plan lessons using a multisensory approach; we must show students that *using those same methods during study time at home* will help them concentrate more and increase their retention of material. They need to learn that when studying they should speak, write, simulate, draw and manipulate. These strategies allow students to process information more completely by more fully engaging them with the material. The "active" study strategies modeled and practiced in school should be reinforced through assignments requiring their application at home. Scores of opportunities must be provided for students to practice using different strategies during study at home. Encourage students to provide concrete evidence that they did, in fact, study. Be sure to have students discuss what strategies they've tried while studying. Students need time to evaluate which strategies work best for them. This metacognitive approach will help students discover how they think and learn best.

Advance Preparation

Make copies of the following reproducibles:

✔ **"Active" Study Strategies** (*page 23*)
✔ **Nightly Study Log** (*page 27*)
✔ **Study Buddies** (*page 28*)
✔ **Test-Prep Kit** (*page 29*)

In addition, have a large stack of 5- x 8-inch index cards and blank flashcards (these may be small rectangles of cut-up recycled paper).

Strategies

"Active" Study Strategies List

The **"Active" Study Strategies** listed on the next page will be helpful in providing concrete activities for students to use at home. The result of almost every one of the strategies described can be brought back to school, so teachers can verify their students' work. Have your students attach this list of strategies to their notebooks for reference at home. Tell them to add new ideas in the space provided as they learn them throughout the year.

"Active" Study Strategies

When studying, I should **RECITE**. I might:

◆ describe or explain aloud any topic, in my own words,

◆ teach or explain the information to someone else (or record into a tape recorder) or,

◆ engage in a simulation or role-play a part.

When studying, I should **WRITE**. I might:

◆ make a Chapter Study Review Card (use an index card; include special vocabulary, main ideas, examples, key events and people, causes, results and so on),

◆ make and use a set of flashcards (vocabulary and definitions, math problems and solutions, questions and answers and so on),

◆ make lists of related information by categories (causes, results, important events or concepts, main ideas, examples, key people and so on) and recite them,

◆ draw a diagram, map, a sketch, or a chart; do this from memory and check your notes or books for accuracy,

◆ write questions I think will be on the test and recite the answers,

◆ create "semantic maps" to summarize the unit; include: Venn diagrams, sequence chains, charts and webs,

◆ create a mnemonic to remember information (such as: **P**lease **E**xcuse **M**y **D**ear **A**unt **S**ally, used for order of operation in solving an equation—**P**arenthesis-**E**xponent-**M**ultiply-**D**ivide-**A**dd-**S**ubtract)

When studying, I should **VISUALIZE**. I might:

◆ close my eyes and "picture in my mind" any chart, diagram, word, map, event, time period, scene, experiment or character (from a story) that I am trying to remember.

When studying, I should_____

_____

_____

_____

Nightly Study Log

Encourage students to use and record one or two "active" techniques each night. You might choose to use the **Nightly Study Log** for a couple of weeks at the beginning of each semester so students will become familiar with trying out different study techniques. After that, you might continue to use the Log with students who are having difficulty learning content curriculum. Ask parents to sign the sheet indicating they have seen their children engaged in the "active" strategies.

Chapter Study Review Cards

Chapter Study Review Cards (see the examples on this page) are an excellent way to summarize information. This strategy is a concrete way for a student to review a chapter and create a study tool for future use as well. Visual learners will enjoy creating and designing these cards to include drawings and symbols, as well as words. Auditory learners will find these cards useful for triggering memory when they recite the information on them at study time. On the blank side of the card the student fills in the title of the chapter in the center of a web. Using a textbook or notebook, he or she records the chapter subtopics on the spokes of the web. (At this point, you can ask that students complete the rest of the activity either at home or with a Study Buddy (see page 25).) On the lined side of the card, the students list additional information about the subtopics.

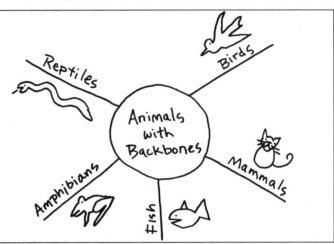

These cards can be used to study for upcoming tests. You might choose to save and store them, returning them to students before a midterm or final exam.

Flashy Review

Traditionally, flashcards have been used to practice vocabulary, with one side recording the word and the other side stating the definition. However, flashcards can also be used to help students make meaningful connections during independent study. When reviewing a chapter or topic, hand out 10 to 20 blank flashcards. Have students write one key word or phrase concerning the topic (name of a person, place, event, object, cause, result, concept and so on) on each flashcard. Next, ask students to group words that are related to one another. (Students will form different groupings because they will see different relationships among the words.) Finally, let students work in pairs to define the words, explain the significance of each to the topic and then relate why they grouped the words in a particular way. During this explanation, students will be making meaningful connections and processing the material more thoroughly. (An easy way to encourage students to make connections after defining the words is by having them create one sentence using all of the words included in a group. An example might be, *The pioneers moving westward in the 1800s had to overcome many difficulties, such as lack of food and water, rough terrain and Indian attacks.*) Students should be prompted to use this strategy at home by reciting aloud. Label and store the chapter flashcards in a zip-top bag or an envelope. Encourage students to use them for review before any exam.

Study Buddies

Encouraging students to study in pairs can help them to increase their understanding of how to study. A week before an upcoming test, have your students choose a partner, and then give them the **Study Buddies** form. The students' job is to list the best "active" study techniques they can think of to learn and process the information that will be on the test. Each student brings to this activity his or her own ideas of how to learn. What is normally an individual and, often, a limited approach to studying, now becomes a shared process for learning. By mixing partners each time you form study buddies, you increase the likelihood that students will gain new strategies. Usually, the planning and the sharing of ideas for study will take place in the classroom and the actual studying will be done at home by each individual. If class time allows, study buddies can engage in peer tutoring or create a study tool. Spend time discussing the ideas generated by the pairs. After an exam, it is worthwhile to ask students which strategies seemed to help the most. (With older students, you may want to change the name "Study Buddies" to "Study Partners.")

Test-Prep Kit

The **Test-Prep Kit** will help students plan independently for an upcoming test. It will encourage them to think about the topic and subtopics of a chapter, take responsibility for learning about the format of the test and make plans for using "active" strategies during multiple study sessions.

Ticket to the Test

Require a "Ticket to the Test." Have students bring some example of their "active" studying to class on the day of a test. Examples of "active" study may include: a new set of flashcards, a list of important definitions from the unit, a study review card, a newly created mnemonic device, a chart or semantic map, a written summary of the unit, a list of questions the student thinks will be on the exam, a tape or parent note indicating the child engaged in reciting during study. Some teachers give bonus points for bringing in the "active" strategies. Others make the strategies a required part of the test worth five or ten points. Still others, occasionally, allow students to use their study tools during the test. This encourages students to create the best study tools they can.

Teaching Suggestions and Extension Ideas

1. Take class time to discuss all the possibilities for studying "actively." Be sure to add your own tips for learning. List and post all of the ideas at the front of the room. Leave space for students to add new ideas as they learn them throughout the year. When announcing an upcoming test, choose one of the strategies to model for students and then provide time for students to practice using it. After several months of practicing assigned strategies, allow students to choose whichever strategies they prefer to prepare for exams. Always take time to evaluate how effective each strategy was in helping them learn the information.

2. In reading classes you could use the Flashy Review to help students to develop a better understanding of a piece of literature. Have students make seven cards labeled: Main Characters, Setting, Theme, Plot, Conflict, Climax and Conclusion. Another card is labeled with the title of the piece of literature the students have just read. Pairs of students describe or explain as much as possible about each of the parts of the story. Partner A begins by describing the Main Characters. Then Partner B adds or suggests changes in the description. After both partners agree on the information (they may have to go back to the reading to prove their points), Partner B begins to describe the Setting. Partner A adds or suggests changes in the description. In this way, the process continues until they have used all seven cards. As a final review, students may write an essay based on their discussions.

For students to compare two pieces of literature, use the seven cards and add two additional cards labeled with the titles of both pieces of literature. Partner A describes the Main Characters in the first piece. Partner B compares those characters to the characters in the second piece. Then, Partner B describes the setting in the second piece and Partner A compares that setting to the setting in the first piece. The process continues until all seven parts of the story have been compared. As a final review, students may choose to create a Venn diagram.

3. When encouraging students to develop study tools to improve memory, *drawing* should not be overlooked or minimized. Using right-, as well as, left-brain approaches to study are likely to increase retention of information. Even if students are not artistic, they can use drawings to help trigger memories of a great deal of information. For example, students studying the American Revolution might be aided in their review by drawing pictures of a British stamp to help them remember the various ways in which Britain tried to control the colonies and to regulate colonial trade. Encourage students to share their drawings with the class.

Nightly Study Log *Week of* _____

"Active" study techniques include:

- ◆ making lists of related information
- ◆ making a study review card
- ◆ making and using a set of flashcards
- ◆ writing questions I think will be on the test
- ◆ drawing a map, sketch, chart or other diagram
- ◆ creating a "semantic map" to organize information
- ◆ reciting important information by explaining or describing in my own words

DAY	SUBJECT/TOPIC	"ACTIVE" TECHNIQUES
		1. 2.
		1. 2.
		1. 2.
		1. 2.
		1. 2.

Parent's Signature _____

Study Buddies

You are having a test next _____ on the following topic:_____.

With your study buddy, plan 3 study sessions over the next week, including as many "active" study techniques as you can.

Study Session 1	Study Session 2	Study Session 3

Test-Prep Kit

Day/Date of test: _____

Topic of the test: _____

Five main ideas about the topic (important concepts, key ideas, causes, results, important events or people):
1.   4.
2.   5.
3.

Ten important terms (vocabulary words) related to the topic:
1.   6.
2.   7.
3.   8.
4.   9.
5.   10.

On the back of this page, write 15 questions you think the teacher will ask on the test.

Ask your teacher about the test, and check off which of the following you should include in your review:
____ class notes   ____ teacher review sheets
____ text readings   ____ past quizzes and tests
____ handouts/dittos/worksheets   ____ other: _____

What format will the test follow:
____ short answer (true-false, multiple choice, fill-in, matching, and so on)
____ essay
____ labeling a picture (a map, parts of a plant, the water cycle and so on)

Check off how many study sessions you will set aside to prepare for the exam:
____ 2 sessions   _____ 3 sessions

Write which days you will study: _____ _____ _____

Check off which "active" study strategies you plan to use in preparation for the test:
____ reciting the main ideas   ____ creating a "semantic map"
____ making a study review card   ____ creating a mnemonic device
____ making and using a set of   ____ drawing a time line
     flashcards   ____ making lists of related information
____ drawing a map, sketch or   ____ other: _____
     other diagram

Chapter 3

Self-Evaluation and Goal Setting

Assessing Progress

Background

For students to "own" their work, they must have a sense that they are in control. They must know that if they perform certain actions, certain things will occur. Encourage students to think in these terms: *If I make a plan to complete my project, I will get it done on time; if I take good notes in class, I will have something to study for my test; if I hand in all my homework, I will earn a better grade for the semester.* Students will need many opportunities to evaluate their behavior and ensuing results. They must be able to assess their own progress in school, set goals for improvement and take responsibility for the results of their efforts. The focus should be on what students can do to improve their study habits and overcome any obstacles in the way of their success.

Advance Preparation

Help students assemble a Learning Log Journal, which will be attached to the inside of a Study Smart Folder. Provide them with folders. To make the journals, have them staple five pieces of lined paper to the left-hand side of the folder. Store these Study Smart Folders in a file organizer or drawer in the classroom. In addition to housing the Learning Log Journal, the Folder will be used throughout the year to file all self-evaluations, contracts and written goals.

Prepare copies of the following reproducibles:

✔ **My Daily Checklist** (*page 34*)
✔ **Blank Checklist** (*page 35*)
✔ **Weekly Self-Evaluation** (*page 36*)
✔ **Report Card Evaluation and Contract** (*page 37*)
✔ **Positive Study Behaviors** (*page 38*)

Strategies

My Learning Log Journal

Have your students write in their Learning Log Journals for five minutes a week about how they are learning, studying or becoming more responsible for their school-work. Encourage them to assess their progress by writing anything that comes to mind or by choosing one of the openings in the box below.

One new thing I tried this week was_____

My goal for next week is_____

To help me remember what I read in my textbook, I_____

Some strategies I can use to study for tests are_____

A few things I can do to make my notebook more organized and useful to me are _____

_____

In order to stay organized and in control of my schoolwork, each night I will _____

_____

My Daily Checklist

Use **My Daily Checklist** to help students start off the year with good study habits. The sample checklist will enable students to evaluate their homework skills. Each day the student checks five behaviors that should become second nature to him or her. Once those habits are in place, use the **Blank Checklist** to include new study behaviors to be learned. The students can evaluate how much effort they are putting into their work by assigning themselves a check, check plus or check minus in the boxes each day.

As an alternative to the Learning Log Journal, have students use the **Weekly Self-Evaluation** form to determine if they have accomplished the actions listed. At the bottom of the page, the student completes open-ended statements and sets a goal for the week. File these self-evaluations in the Study Smart Folder.

The **Report Card Evaluation and Contract** can be used at the end of each marking period to help students evaluate their progress and focus on behaviors they can use to improve grades. A list of **Positive Study Behaviors** is provided to help students be specific about what they can do to improve. You can add to the list by brainstorming with your class about strategies they can use to improve learning. File these evaluation/contracts in the Study Smart Folder. Periodically, check to see that students are moving in a timely fashion toward their goals.

Teaching Suggestions and Extension Ideas

1. Spend class time discussing good study habits. Ask for volunteers to share successes that they've had, obstacles that stand in the way of their performance (sports programs keeping them late after school everyday, sharing a room with siblings and trying to find "quiet time" for homework and so on) and new strategies that they've tried. Have students brainstorm solutions to obstacles. After the discussion, allow a few minutes for students to record the ideas that they want to try in the future in their Learning Log Journals.

2. My Daily Checklist can be used with the entire class or given to a child having specific difficulties. It also may be tailored to meet individual needs.

3. The self-evaluations may be reviewed periodically by students and new goals set. If parent conferences are held, the self-evaluations will provide parents with insight about the behaviors they should be observing at home.

My Daily Checklist

	M	T	W	T	F
I carefully copied down my homework assignment.					
I brought home all needed material to do my assignment.					
I began my homework at a set time. (_____)time					
I put 100% effort into completing my homework carefully and neatly.					
When I finished I placed my homework in my homework/travel folder and put the folder in my backpack or bookbag.					

Parent's Signature _____

My Daily Checklist

	M	T	W	T	F

Parent's Signature _____

Weekly Self-Evaluation

Name_____

Check if accomplished

This week I

❑ studied in a **quiet environment.**

❑ used a **study schedule** (to plan several study sessions for an upcoming test).

❑ made or used a **weekly schedule** (to plan/keep track of long-term assignments).

❑ **turned off** the **radio or television** when I was studying.

❑ **recorded homework assignments** on a pad or on one page in my notebook.

❑ **completed all homework** assignments.

❑ **organized my schoolwork** (using folders, cleaning out my book bag/desk/locker).

❑ studied my **most difficult subject first** (or second).

❑ **studied earlier** in the day (whenever I could).

❑ added a **"study period"** after homework was completed.

❑ used **"active" study techniques** (including reciting, making flashcards, taking notes, listing, drawing, visualizing, making up test questions).

❑ **listened** more **carefully** in class.

❑ **participated actively** during class discussions.

❑ **took some form of notes** during each class.

❑ **"actively" reviewed my class notes each night** (to increase retention).

❑ **prepared for upcoming tests** by using "active" study techniques in study sessions.

Complete the following statements.

Something new that worked well for me this week was:_____

I tried hard to:_____

I have begun to see positive results in:_____

I feel good about:_____

I have put more effort into:_____

This week my goal is to:_____
(be specific)

Report Card Evaluation and Contract to Improve My Grades

Name _____ Date _____

This past semester my grades for this class were: _____

I earned these grades because:

_____   I completed all assignments.

_____   I met all deadlines.

_____   I came to class prepared to learn.

_____   I participated actively and cooperatively during class discussions.

_____   I studied effectively for tests.

_____   I did not complete all assignments.

_____   I handed work in late.

_____   I frequently was unprepared.

_____   I did not contribute in a positive way to class discussions.

_____   I did not study effectively for tests.

_____   other: _____.

I would like to bring my grade(s) up to: _____

In order to improve my grade(s), I will:

1.   6.

2.   7.

3.   8.

4.   9.

5.   10.

I, _____, hereby, sign this contract to improve my grades, knowing full well that I am responsible for the grades I receive. I have the power to improve my grades by changing my study behaviors.

I pledge to review this contract once a week to make sure that I am following the steps necessary to reach my goal by the end of this semester.

Optional: My parents and I agree that if I reach my goal, I will reward myself in the following way: _____

Parent's Signature _____

Teacher's Signature _____

Positive Study Behaviors

Choose from the following list of positive study behaviors when setting goals for yourself:

In Class
✔ **Listen** carefully to the teacher.
✔ **Avoid talking to friends** during class instruction.
✔ Practice **taking** better **notes.**
✔ **Write down assignments** and due dates carefully.
✔ **Participate actively** in class discussions.
✔ **Ask the teacher questions** when I don't understand.

At Home
✔ Set a **"Study time"** separate from homework time.
✔ **Study** more **frequently,** for shorter time periods. (Four half-hour study sessions are much better than one two-hour session.)
✔ Study my **most difficult subject early** in my study session.
✔ Use **"active"** study techniques (recite, write, visualize, make study review cards and so on).
✔ **Review class notes each night** by reciting or writing marginal notes or questions (to increase retention).
✔ **Organize** myself **each night for the next day** (file papers, check schedule and calendar and weekly goals).

Time Management
✔ Make a **study schedule** over the weekend for the following week.
✔ **Begin to study at the time I have planned** to do so.
✔ **Study earlier** in the day (before dinner) whenever possible.
✔ **Use** some **weekend time** for studying if I get home late on school nights because of school sports.
✔ **Use a calendar** for recording due dates and **setting "weekly goals."**
✔ **Break large assignments into smaller parts** and set deadlines for finishing each part. **Use the calendar.**

Study Environment
✔ Study in a **quiet** environment.
✔ Study the **same subject** in the **same place** at the **same time** each day.
✔ **Organize** my desk, drawers and paper. (Use folders.)
✔ **Remove visual distractions** from my study location.
✔ **Provide enough light** to read by without strain.
✔ **Have all materials** I need for homework or study **nearby** (paper, ruler, tape, stapler, dictionary and so on)
✔ Put up a **bulletin board** where I can post a calendar, schedule, reminder cards and so on.

Chapter 4

Better Note Taking

Getting It All Down

Background

Although there is no one best way to take notes, research suggests that the very act of note taking, in any form, promotes retention of information. Note taking increases concentration. It helps the individual to organize, process and encode information and it provides material for the student to study later on.

High school teachers expect their students to be able to take notes during class, but that assumes a great deal. Where and when have students been given the instruction and repeated opportunities for practicing note taking? Instruction in organizing notebooks and recording topics that have been studied can begin early in elementary school. Even students in second and third grade can be shown how to label and date any work recorded in their notebooks. Teaching this habit early will make keeping notes organized later much easier.

Most of what goes on in classrooms is auditory. The teacher introduces a topic or leads the class through an activity. Students discuss their experiments, describe steps in solving a math problem or respond verbally to something they have read. Since most of our students are visual learners, this method of instruction does not match their learning style. It is imperative, therefore, that we help students take the great amount of auditory input received during class and transcribe it into some visual form.

Be sure to model several note-taking strategies during the course of the year. Additional opportunities for practice should be provided, both during class and for homework, in order for students to use and improve this skill.

I have included on the next page a suggested scope and sequence of subskills for the middle grades which will lead to improved note taking later on. While I will illustrate several methods of note taking, I will provide many suggestions for using a favorite note taking strategy of mine, the Cornell Method, or Column Note Taking.

Toward Better Note Taking —
A Suggested Scope and Sequence

Key: I - Introduce/Model frequently
T - Teach (provide many opportunities for student practice)
R - Review (extend, students apply independently when developmentally ready)

4	5	6	7	8	Grades
					Getting Started:
I	I	T	T	R	Writes title/heading on page correctly
I	I	T	T	R	Labels all notes in notebook-date, topic, page
I	I	T	T	R	Leaves a wide 3" margin (recall column)
I	I	T	T	R	Skips lines between subtopics
I	I	T	T	R	Copies all notes accurately off board, leaving a wide margin on the left
	I	I	T	T	After copying notes off board, can generate questions in the recall column
	I	I	T	T	Circles and underlines key phrases in notebook when studying
					From Text:
I	I	I	T	T	Can paraphrase a paragraph that has been read
I	I	I	T	T	Can describe a sequence of events, steps, or ideas
	I	I	T	T	Can list main ideas/subtopics
	I	I	T	T	Can list details for each main idea/subtopic
	I	I	T	T	Can make a "semantic map" which shows main ideas/subtopics
	I	I	T	T	Can categorize details under subtopics
		I	I	I	Can write a summary of a section
					From Classroom Discussion:
		I	I		Can paraphrase what has been said
		I	I		Can describe a sequence of events, steps, or ideas
		I	I		Can list main ideas/subtopics
		I	I		Can list details for each main idea /subtopics
		I	I		Can make a "semantic map" which shows main ideas/subtopics
		I	I		Can write a summary
		I	I		Can use a "semantic map" to outline an essay with three main ideas/subtopics and two details for each
			I		Can identify the speaker's or writer's organizational plan, such as: simple listing, chronological pattern, cause and effect, generalization with examples, comparison and contrast

Advance Preparation

As you prepare for each unit of study (your content curriculum), develop several examples of note-taking strategies based on upcoming class assignments to model on the overhead or blackboard.

Have on hand copies of the following reproducibles:

✔ **K-W-L Chart** (*page 46*)
✔ **Topic-Subtopics Map** (*page67*)
✔ **Noting What I've Learned** (*page 47*)
✔ **Column Note Taking Outlines** (*pages 48 and 49*)

Strategies

The Traditional Outline

Traditional outlining is really quite an advanced concept that requires students to use many higher-level thinking skills. Among other things, it assumes students can use complex organizational skills. Most students in the middle grades will not be developmentally ready to use this strategy effectively on their own.

If you choose to introduce this form of note taking, you will need to walk students through the process step-by-step, always modeling your own notes on the overhead or blackboard. Students will need a great deal of guidance as they begin to identify the various parts of an outline.

In my opinion, the strategies below are simpler and more effective for most students.

K-W-L Chart

A **K-W-L Chart** can help students relate what they already know about a topic to the new information they are about to learn. It is through connections that we make meaning from what we learn and improve the likelihood that we can retrieve the information later from our memory. The chart may be used to record new information gathered through research, class discussion, viewing films or reading the textbook.

Mapping

Most students prefer creating semantic maps to using traditional notes and outlines. A map, or graphic organizer, is a visual representation of ideas that the student organizes and designs. (See Chapter 9, *Learning Through Visualization*, for more information on graphic organizers.) Main ideas are attached to the topic and details are attached to the main ideas. This "word map" show relationships of concepts to one another. The **Topic-Subtopics Map** trains students to think critically as they judge how ideas are related to one another and which ideas are more important than others (main ideas vs. details.) Creating maps helps students integrate the thinking-reading-writing processes.

For students to commit themselves to creating and designing maps during study time, they need to be convinced of the maps' usefulness. To accomplish this, provide students with a map you have created of an upcoming unit. They should not be familiar with the material. Have students in pairs discuss what they can learn from the map. Then, as a class, ask them to share what the pairs have learned. Discuss whether a map would be useful for taking notes from future textbook assignments. Most students will admit that they learned a great deal from your map. They will, therefore, be more eager to try it out as a study tool for themselves.

Noting What I've Learned

The easiest form of note taking for a student is to write a simple list of new ideas that he or she has learned. Usually, the list has no particular form, but it provides a record of important facts. Using the **Noting What I've Learned** outline, you can provide a structure for a simple list. Discuss the general topic of an assigned reading with your students and have them record the topic on the top of the page. Since this is probably a first experience with note taking, present students with three or four subtopics included in their assignment. Have them write the subtopics in the boxes provided. As they read the assignment, students should record two or three details (definitions, explanations, examples and so on) about each subtopic. A completed outline is shown below. Students also will enjoy drawing pictures in the boxes to aid visual memory.

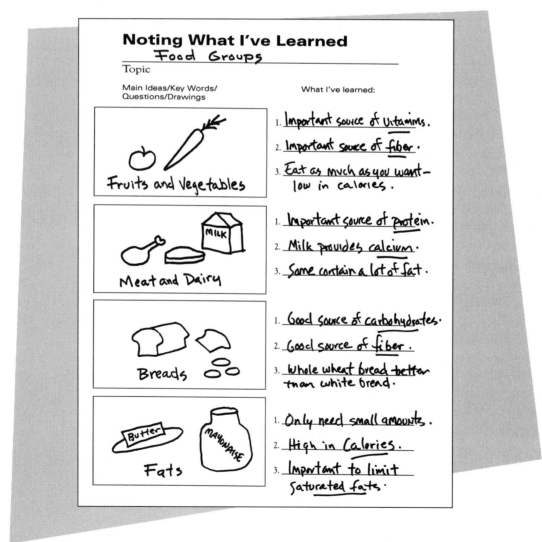

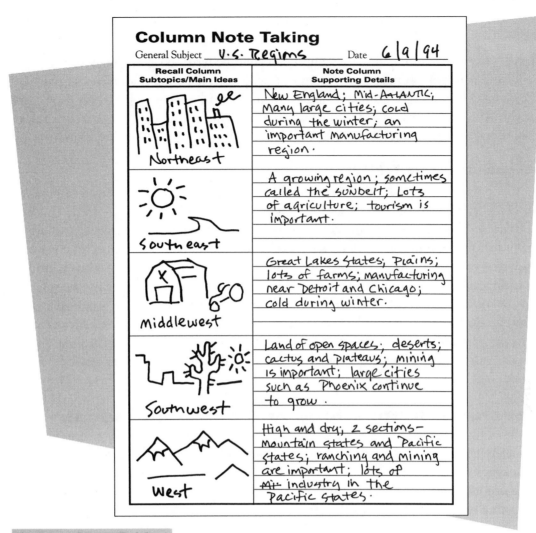

Column Note Taking

General Subject ___U·S· Regions___ Date __6|9|94__

Recall Column Subtopics/Main Ideas	Note Column Supporting Details
Northeast	New England; Mid-Atlantic; Many large cities; cold during the winter; an important manufacturing region.
Southeast	A growing region; sometimes called the sunbelt; Lots of agriculture; tourism is important.
Middlewest	Great Lakes States; Plains; lots of farms; manufacturing near Detroit and Chicago; cold during winter.
Southwest	Land of open spaces; deserts; cactus and plateaus; mining is important; large cities such as Phoenix continue to grow.
West	High and dry; 2 sections— mountain states and Pacific states; ranching and mining are important; lots of industry in the Pacific states.

Column Note Taking

My favorite note-taking strategy is adapted from Walter Pauk's Cornell Method, Column Note Taking. Developed for college students, this method calls for students to take notes on the right-hand side of the page in the Note Column. Afterwards, they create marginal comments, questions or key phrases which they record in the left-hand column, called the Recall Column. This is one of the most effective note-taking strategies because it provides an excellent independent study tool for students. By covering the Note Column, students can quiz themselves by reciting information triggered by notes in the Recall Column. By uncovering the Note Column they can get immediate feedback about the accuracy and completeness of their memory.

I have adapted the **Column Note Taking** outline for a variety of purposes. The form on page 48 has boxes in the Recall Column which can be used in many ways. Main ideas, questions, drawings, key words and problems can be written in the boxes. Pictures can be drawn to illustrate key ideas. A description of the picture can be written in the Note Column. In Science classes, students can draw what they observe at different stages in an experiment, and then write a description in the Note Column. Language Arts and English teachers like to use the boxes to list literary terms. Math teachers have used the boxes to write word problems which their students solve on the line to the right. Above is a completed sample from a Social

Studies class. A summarizing paragraph can then be written on the back of the page.

Using the form on page 49, students can copy or take their own notes in the Note Column. After doing so, they can generate and record questions based on their notes in the Recall Column. Younger or less able students can decide what the notes are describing and they can label the main idea or subtopic in the Recall Column.

Cooperative Note Taking

Cooperative note-taking activities help students learn new ideas from one another. Provide frequent opportunities for students to take notes. One way to do this is to prepare a five-minute lecture (be sure your presentation is organized, including: three to four subtopics with details for each). Have students listen and take notes in the right column (using **Column Note Taking**). After the lecture, ask each student to individually spend five minutes clarifying his or her notes and writing questions or key words and concepts in the Recall Column. Then have pairs of students discuss what they have noted and how each partner has organized the information. Encourage students to borrow at least one idea from their partner's notes. As a class, discuss the process of note taking while the teacher shows his/her notes for the lecture on the overhead or blackboard.

Teaching Suggestions and Extension Ideas

1. Remember when you review the Suggested Scope and Sequence that developmentally there will be a great range of abilities within one grade level. You and your colleagues need not be locked into the exact time frame suggested. Instead, review your unique school population and its needs, and just be sure to build upon the sub-skills in a unified approach for the best long-term outcomes.

2. The **K-W-L Chart** is especially helpful at the 4–6 grade level. Using it at the beginning of each new unit of study will activate prior knowledge and provide motivation to investigate a topic further. Some students will resist and say, "I don't *want* to know anything more." In that case, smile, change the **W** to an **N** and ask, "What do you *need* to know? in order to fully understand the topic?"

3. The **Noting What I've Learned** outline can be used in any classroom. For example, in Science and Art classes, students can record information about equipment, safety, steps to follow, ingredients, types of materials and so on. They can draw pictures in the boxes to help them remember the way things should look. A summary can be written as a follow-up.

In Social Studies, Science, and Health classes students can prepare brief oral reports to present to the class. Insist that the reports be organized and include three to four subtopics/main ideas with two or three details for each. Student listeners at their desks can take notes using this outline. A summary of one of the reports can be written for homework with students using only what is recorded in the notes.

In English classes, students can employ this outline to keep track of information when they prepare for a book report. Tell them to staple two outlines together and label each box with the parts of a story, such as, Main Characters, Setting, Theme,

Conflict, Resolution and so on. As students read, they can record details that are related to each part. Younger students can draw pictures in the boxes which illustrate important events or ideas from the book. Details about the picture can be noted to the right.

4. In addition to the many suggestions given for using **Column Note Taking**, one additional strategy comes to mind which has broad applications among the varied disciplines. After your class has completed reading a piece of literature from a particular time period or culture or a chapter from a text, have students generate a random list of important ideas and concepts gleaned from the reading. Record these ideas and concepts on the blackboard. Then pair off the students and have them group the ideas by category (family customs, food, education, daily life, geography and so on.) Instruct them to use Column Note Taking and record the categories, or subtopics, in the Recall Column, and the specific ideas and concepts in the Note Column.

5. The best way to benefit from note taking is to interact with the notes *soon after taking them.* Visual learners should be encouraged to write marginal notes or questions as they review their notes nightly. They can use highlighters to emphasize important information, draw boxes around key concepts and enumerate details listed. Occasionally, you should ask them to transcribe their notes into some other form (a chart, Venn diagram, matrix, summary and so on) for homework. Auditory learners should be encouraged to recite the information from their notes. They can use a tape recorder if that makes it more fun, or they can simply close their door and pretend they are teaching someone else. Long-term memory is increased by engaging in *review soon after the first exposure* to information.

6. Another way to engage students in cooperative note-taking activities is to prepare another five-minute lecture. (Again, be sure your presentation is organized and includes three to four subtopics with details for each). Students listen and take notes in any form (simple listing, Column Note Taking, Mapping, Traditional Outlining and so on). After the lecture, each individual spends five minutes editing, clarifying, reorganizing the notes. Then students switch papers. Each student writes a summary—using only what is provided in the notes. Do not grade these papers. Use them only as a means of identifying the best note-taking strategies. Discuss which type of note taking led to the most complete summary. Provide frequent opportunities to try again.

(Topic) _____

K

(List what you already **know** about the topic.)

W

(List questions about what you **want to know** about the topic.)

L

(Using your questions as a guide, write all the information you have **learned** in this column. Use the back of this page if necessary.)

Noting What I've Learned

Topic _____

Main Ideas/Key Words/ Questions/Drawings	What I've learned:
	1. _____ 2. _____ 3. _____
	1. _____ 2. _____ 3. _____
	1. _____ 2. _____ 3. _____
	1. _____ 2. _____ 3. _____

Column Note Taking

General Subject _____ Date _____

Recall Column Subtopics/Main Ideas	Note Column Supporting Details

Column Note Taking

General Subject _____ Date _____

Recall Column Subtopics/Main Ideas	Note Column Supporting Details

Chapter 5

Getting More Out of Textbook Assignments

Making Sense of the Reading

Background

A typical textbook assignment asks students to read a certain number of pages and answer some questions. The approach most students use in completing such assignments is to read the questions and skim through the chapter to locate and record the answers. Little meaning is gleaned from the assignment, as students simply are finding isolated facts and making few connections. This chapter will focus on strategies which require students to interact more fully with the text, thereby greatly increasing their comprehension of the material. It will suggest activities for students to use *before* being given an assignment, activities to minimize passivity *during* an assignment and activities which teach students to process information immediately *after* an assignment. In addition, the chapter will provide opportunities for students to learn to use the text as a valuable resource tool.

Advance Preparation

Have on hand copies of the following reproducibles:

✔ **Advance Organizer** (*page 55*)
✔ **SQ3R** (*page 56*)
✔ **Text Learning Strategy** (*page 57*)
✔ **Guided Reading Assignment** (*page 58*)
✔ **Peer Teaching Plan** (*page 59*)

Strategies

Before giving textbook assignments:

Textbook Scavenger Hunt

Have a "Textbook Scavenger Hunt" so students can familiarize themselves with the unique parts of their text. Students will learn to find information in all parts of their book and discover that texts are valuable resource tools to be used throughout the year.

Chapter Prediction

For homework assign a Chapter Prediction. Tell students to look over the visual aids in the chapter such as pictures, charts, diagrams and tables. Have them write a paragraph about what they think the main ideas of the chapter will be. This exercise will help provide a purpose for reading. The visuals will help students recall information later.

An Advance Organizer

Advance organizers are prereading aids which help students make connections between what they already know and what they are about to learn. Unlimited in possibilities, advance organizers can be written or verbal. They include any effort on the part of the teacher to link new material to concepts already understood. For example, any prior presentation of main ideas and key concepts, a K-W-L Chart (see page 46), a list of words students will encounter, a paraphrased explanation of the reading or questions posed to motivate and focus the reader—are all examples of advance organizers. Students will need the opportunity to respond to the advance organizer in order to make connections for themselves. Students can use the **Advance Organizer for Textbook Assignment** to help them approach a textbook reading in a more active and thoughtful way.

During an assignment:

SQ3R

After reading Francis Robinson's method of reading a text, known as **SQ3R**, have students complete short reading assignments following the prescribed steps. By using the steps of Survey, Question, Read, Recite, Review, your students will be engaged actively in their reading. Their comprehension and recall will improve greatly and the notes they take following this method will be useful for studying for tests later.

Questioning Everything: A Paragraph-by-Paragraph Approach

Have students draw a vertical line three inches from the left edge of a page in their notebook. Have them label this column *Questions*. Then have them label the right-hand column *Notes*. After assigning one or two pages of reading, ask students to write a question in the *Questions* column for each paragraph they read. First, be sure to model questions that show higher-level thinking and questions that focus on the main idea of a paragraph. Require students to answer each question in the *Notes* column to the right of the question. Instruct them to skip lines between each answer.

This question-answer note taking will serve as an independent study tool later when, by covering answers with a piece of paper, the students can test their recall of important information and get immediate feedback regarding their knowledge.

Text Learning Strategy

Based on Donald Dansereau's cooperative learning script, this strategy will lead students to better individual studying. Have students work in pairs with the task to teach one another the information in a text reading. They will follow the steps on the **Text Learning Strategy** "script" to help them focus both on the content of the reading and the process of learning.

Text Study Guide

A Text Study Guide provides students with a step-by-step guide to help them proceed through a reading assignment. Once students become familiar with such an approach, they can use similar steps to read any text assignment. See the sample on this page for the kinds of instructions you might use.

Guided Reading Assignment

As an alternative to the Text Study Guide, students can use the **Guided Reading Assignment** which has them focus on the main ideas, details, sequence of information, visual typographical aids and overall presentation of material.

After an assignment:

Chapter Study Review Cards

After your class has completed reading a textbook chapter using the suggestions above, invite them to create a Chapter Study Review Card (see Chapter 2). Students can use these cards during independent study for reciting and self-testing. An entire unit can be reduced to one to three index cards. Two holes may be punched in the cards so students can keep them in their binders.

Text Study Guide
The American Nation

Chapter 19
Section 2: The President and Congress Clash
pp. 421-425

Page

425: Read the "Section Review" first. Note that you are starting at the end of the chapter with the summary questions. These questions will give you a purpose for reading. When you read your assignment, your mind will be seeking answers to these questions.

421: Next, read the "Read to Learn" section. This is the introductory section. It will prepare your mind to pick up certain information as you read. Jot down important questions, names, concepts or vocabulary words you will be reading about. Skip lines. Identify later as you read.

Write down the two main goals of the "Radical Republicans."

423: Describe the Fourteenth Amendment.

Describe the conflict between Congress and the President

424: The italicized word must be important. Copy it. Define it. Why did the Republicans try to impeach President Johnson?

425: Stop here and write a two-sentence summary of the chapter so far.

Although peer teaching takes a good deal of time, it, nevertheless, remains one of the most effective learning strategies. As teachers, we can attest to the fact that when we have to teach something to others, we learn the material well. Using this principle, the **Peer Teaching Plan** will help students become facile with any information as they prepare to teach it to others.

Teaching Suggestions and Extension Ideas

1. When using the Text Scavenger Hunt, be sure to have examples that include the title, author, copyright date (is the information new or dated?), table of contents, glossary, index and chapter format (chapter objectives, section review and so on). Use this strategy when you first hand out the text, and then plan to use a variation of it periodically as a warm-up. This will keep students familiar with their text as a resource tool.

2. Have students take notes as they read a textbook assignment using either the Column Note Taking Method (see page 48) or semantic maps (see page 82). Give students credit the next day for bringing complete and organized notes. Pair students off so they can compare the notes they've taken. Model good note taking by choosing good examples from students and putting them on the overhead projector to discuss.

3. Have students jot down 10 to 15 new pieces of information that they glean from their reading. Discuss the concept of main ideas vs. details. Ask students to record main ideas rather than details.

4. Try to integrate any music or art that might relate to a period you are reading about. Visuals make lasting impressions; music can trigger holistic memories.

5. Change the main event in the story, a step in the experiment or an important happening in history and have students predict what might have occurred instead.

6. Pair students and have them prepare an interview with one of the characters in a story or a person from history that they've read about in their textbook.

7. Ask pairs or small groups of students to create a newspaper front page about a story or period in history. The page could include a factual article, an interview with a character or important person, a "famous" quote (created by the students), a Venn diagram, a sequence chain or flow chart.

8. Have students create a flip chart book which summarizes the reading or experiment. Pictures with captions should describe events or steps from the beginning, the middle and the end. These flip chart books could serve as advance organizers for future classes learning about the same topic.

9. Let groups of students prepare a Student News Show to present to the class. The main ideas of a particular unit or reading must be included. Students can dress up as famous characters or persons from history. The show might include interviews, demonstrations, "historical" commercials and visuals created to support news segments.

Advance Organizer for Textbook Assignment

Today's reading will be about: (Paraphrased explanation of the reading)

_____

_____

_____

_____

Main Ideas/Key Concepts to Be Found In The Reading:
1.

2.

3.

4.

Important Terms to Be Familiar With:

1.   6.

2.   7.

3.   8.

4.   9.

5.   10.

Focus Questions to Consider:
1.

2.

3.

4.

5.

On the back of this page, write **what you already know about this topic.**
On the spokes of a wheel (like the one below) record any
ideas you already have about today's reading.

Using SQ3R For Textbook Reading

S Survey

Spend the first three to four minutes previewing the chapter. Skim the whole assignment, noting the bold face print, chapter headings, subheadings and italicized words. Look at any charts, pictures, graphs or other visual material and read the caption below. Briefly read any introductory paragraphs and summary sections. Note any glossary terms listed.

You should now have an idea about what you will be reading. Understanding the overall plan will help you organize and store the information in your mind as you read through the assignment.

Q Question

For each section of the chapter, write a question that you think will be answered. Sometimes you can turn the headings and subheadings into questions. Recognize that the details are there to explain and support the main points. Try to make questions of the main points of the section.

R Read

Read to find the answer to your first question. Stop reading at the end of the section.

R Recite

Looking up from the text, state from memory the answer to your first question. Use your own words and give any examples to support your statements. Jot down your answer in phrases.

(Now repeat the steps **Question, Read,** and **Recite** for each section of the reading. Write a question for the next section, read to find the answer, look up and recite the answer in your own words and jot down key phrases in your notebook for future study. Read in this active way until you complete the assignment.)

R Review

After you have completed the entire lesson, look over your notes briefly. Try to focus on the main points of the reading, asking yourself what is most important about each section. Recite the key points or write a brief summary of the whole reading.

Following this method, you will have feedback as to whether or not you understand what you have read. The immediate review helps to fix ideas in your memory. The brief notes taken will serve as a tool for future study.

Text Learning Strategy

Cooperative Learning Script

1. Flip a coin to determine who will be Partner A and who will be Partner B. (If there is a trio, one becomes Partner A and two become Partners B.)

2. Both partners read Passage I of any reading or Section I of any text.

3. When both of you are finished, put the passage out of sight.

4. Partner A orally **summarizes** the contents of Passage I. He or she discusses **key points** and **identifies main ideas.**

5. Partner B **detects and corrects any errors** in Partner A's summary and points out any important ideas his or her partner left out. Partner B's focus should be on the content.

6. Both partners work together to **develop images, diagrams, semantic maps, lists, charts, mnemonic devices** and so on, to help make the summarized information memorable. They ask themselves, "How can we learn and remember this information?" The focus is on the process of learning.

7. Both partners read Passage II.

8. Partners reverse roles and repeat steps 4–6.

Adapted from: Donald Dansereau *Journal of Reading* April 1987

Guided Reading Assignment

You are about to read an assignment on _____.
Before you begin the reading, look over the questions on this guide. As you read the assignment, notice the visuals and look for answers to the questions.

1. Write a **description of 3 to 4** visual aids included in this chapter (charts, pictures, diagrams and so on)

    1.

    2.

    3.

    4.

2. How well do you **pick out main ideas?** List 3 to 5 main ideas that you read about. How well do you read for **details**? For each main idea you read about, list 2 to 3 details.

    1. Main Idea _____

        1.

        2.

        3.

    2. Main Idea _____

        1.

        2.

        3.

    3. Main Idea _____

        1.

        2.

        3.

    4. Main Idea _____

        1.

        2.

        3.

    5. Main Idea _____

        1.

        2.

        3.

3. How well do you **follow the sequence of information**? List in correct order several events (or steps) described in your reading.

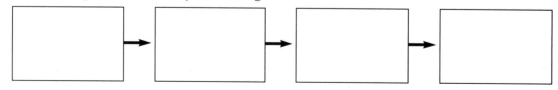

4. How well do you understand **what's most important**? On the back of this page, write a paragraph that **summarizes** what this reading is about.

Peer Teaching Plan

_____ My **topic is:** _____

_____ **Main ideas** I will cover are:

    1.

    2.

    3.

_____ For each main idea above, I will present **two supporting details:**

    Main Idea _____
        1.
        2.
    Main Idea _____
        1.
        2.
    Main Idea _____
        1.
        2.

_____ I will create a **web** to introduce my topic. It will include the topic and subtopics/main ideas. The words will be large enough to be seen by students at their seats.

_____ My **visual** will illustrate one or more of my main ideas. (On the back of this paper, sketch your visual. It can be a chart, drawing, Venn diagram, political map or any other visual you think will be helpful.)

_____ Other **teaching strategies** that I will use during my presentation to the class include:

    _____ Props: _____   _____ Overhead projector
    _____ Lecture   _____ Blackboard
    _____ Demonstration   _____ Other: _____
    _____ Activity: _____   _____

_____ The **follow-up activity** I will develop for the class is:

    _____ a group activity: _____
    _____ a test
    _____ a crossword puzzle
    _____ other: _____

Chapter 6

Better Report Writing

Finding It Out and Putting It All Together

Background

There are several problems that teachers encounter when assigning reports for their classes to do. The first problem is that students have difficulty narrowing down the topic and developing subtopics for their research. Once they begin the research, they have difficulty organizing their notes and synthesizing information from the several sources required. Probably the greatest frustration for teachers is that in the end, the work clearly is not in the students' own words.

Many students need to learn how to spread out their work instead of waiting until the last minute to begin. Students, as well as their parents (who may be involved with transportation to the library or helping to type the final product) will avoid the pressure of having to complete everything in a final rush to meet the deadline by having a plan.

This chapter will focus on strategies to make report writing easier and more productive. The first strategy is a step-by-step method for guiding students through the report process. The "Web Method for Report Writing" described will help students to produce reports that are written in their own words.

Advance Preparation

Have on hand copies of the following reproducibles:

✔ **Project Planner** (*page 79*)
✔ **Monthly Calendar** (*page 80*)
✔ **Parent Report Notice** (*page 66*)
✔ **Topic—Subtopics Web** (*page 67*)
✔ **Web Method For Report Writing** (*page 68*)

Strategies

Step 1 *Time Management*

In order to teach students how to spread out their work on long-term assignments, you must provide many opportunities for them to make up their own plans and schedules. Before they will learn to do this on their own, however, they will need to be shown how and why a schedule works well. To accomplish this, provide students with a **Project Planner**. If the report is due in two or three weeks, you will need to provide two or three planners. Staple them together. Another option is to use the **Monthly Calendar** with its Weekly Goals. (See Chapter 8 on *Time Management* for details about how to use the Project Planner or Monthly Calendar.) Next work with the class to fill in deadlines for each part of the report to be handed in or, at least, checked. Be sure to require several stages of completion, i.e., the Topic-Subtopics Web is due _____, the bibliography is due _____, the detail notes taken are due _____, the rough draft is due _____ and so on.

Although periodically checking student progress on reports might seem time-consuming, it is the only way for students to learn how to do this on their own. Along the way, you should send a **Parent Report Notice** home if any child misses one of the short-term deadlines. In this way, parents will be able to support your efforts to teach students how to make good decisions about the use of time. Ask parents to sign and comment on the notice before returning it to you.

Step 2 *A General Subject Area*

Most teachers assign a report to go along with a unit of study from their curriculum. Thus, many students decide to give reports on "Ancient Egypt," "Energy," "Rocks and Minerals," "Weather," "Mexico," and so on. These topics are often too broad and should have a narrower focus.

Step 3 *Narrowing Down A Topic*

Narrowing the focus requires some familiarity with categories of information about the topic. The researcher must move from one category of information to a class of information within that category.

In order to glean an overview of categories about an unfamiliar topic, students need to skim an encyclopedia, text, general reference book or the *Readers' Guide To Periodical Literature* or scan a computer data base. First, model this process in class by using the **Topic-Subtopics Web**, your text and an encyclopedia. Show students how to find subtopics under a general topic by going through two or three examples. Next, give a list of general topics to your students and have them choose two which interest them. Using the Topics-Subtopics Web, have them narrow the topic through research in the library. This should take approximately thirty minutes because they are not doing the actual research. They are only listing subtopics on their webs. Finally, assign a few general topics for homework and ask students to come up with five or six subtopics on their own. Familiar topics will not require library research, (e.g., Our School; Football; My Life).

Step 4 *Writing A Thesis Statement (Optional)*

Some teachers like their students to develop their reports around a thesis statement. In one or two sentences, the student states a point of view or main idea about the topic. (For example, for a Health class: *One of the most serious problems facing society today is rampant drug abuse*"; or for a Science class: "*Recycling is one of the most important activities for families and communities to engage in if they are to protect future generations.*") All of the student's research is then designed to support his or her viewpoint. The main idea is supported by examples, facts and figures.

Step 5 *Taking Notes and Organizing Them*

Most students first learning how to write reports would find taking notes on cards cumbersome and confusing. A simple, yet effective, way to take notes and stay organized is to use the **Web Method For Report Writing**. It allows students to easily synthesize notes taken from several sources. Not only does this method aid in the organization of the report, but it helps assure that the report will be written in the students' own words.

Provide students with a **Web Method For Report Writing** and a **Topic-Subtopic Web** that has eight spokes. (They may add more or use fewer spokes than provided.) Have them write their topic in the center. Then, after doing preliminary research to narrow their focus, have them write several subtopics (or main ideas) on the spokes. This first web will provide an overview of the report. *This should be the first teacher checkpoint with an assigned deadline.*

After you have checked the direction of the student research by approving the subtopics and/or making additional suggestions, have the students count out one blank web for each subtopic listed on the spokes and staple them behind their first web. (five subtopics=five additional blank webs, and so on.)

Next students should write one subtopic from their overview web in the center of each blank web. They can now begin to research each subtopic and write the details that they learn on the spokes of the appropriate Web.

It is important that you instruct students to **write only phrases or key words on the spokes—no complete sentences should be accepted.** The short lines should encourage this brief note taking. The students then will have to weave together the report in their own words.

Step 6 *Compiling A Bibliography and Using References*

A *bibliography* is a list of sources *found* on the topic. *References* are a list of the sources *used* in the report. If you want the students to keep track of their sources, have them write a list of all the sources they found on a separate piece of paper. Tell them to give a number to each source used. When recording details from a particular source on a Web, tell them to write the number of the reference next to the spoke of the Web.

Step 7   *Writing A "Sloppy Copy" or Rough Draft*

A. *Writing an Introduction*
Explain to students that this where to:
TELL THEM WHAT YOU ARE GOING TO TELL THEM!!

Using the first web, the overview of the report, students should develop an introductory paragraph. The optional thesis statement should serve as a part of the introduction to the report. The paragraph should tell readers what the main ideas are in the report and interest enough to read further.

B. *Writing the Body of the Report*
This is where to:
TELL THEM!!

Each additional web should be developed into a separate paragraph.

C. *Writing a Conclusion*
The conclusion is where to:
TELL THEM WHAT YOU TOLD THEM!!

Have students write a concluding paragraph to summarize their reports.

Step 8   *Editing The "Sloppy Copy" or Rough Draft*
Encourage students to:
A. Check spelling, grammar and expression of ideas.
B. Make sure all required parts of the report, i.e., title page, charts, bibliography, and so on, have been included.
C. Rewrite the "sloppy copy."
D. Proofread the final copy.

Step 9   *Demonstrating What Has Been Learned*
The student should be able to show what he or she has learned by doing the research. A written report is only one way of accomplishing that. Another strategy is to require each student to teach others about the chosen topic. A brief oral report can be assigned where the student is expected to teach new information to the rest of the class. Each presentation must be accompanied by a fact sheet which can be handed out or a large visual which illustrates the main points of the research.

Setting up an exhibition is a little more time-consuming, but is probably one of the most effective strategies for demonstrating what has been learned. Each student becomes the "expert" on his or her own topic and other students and/or parents are invited to visit the exhibitions to hear about the topic and view visual material and artifacts gathered or created. The students who listen can record information for a variety of purposes. They can help evaluate the students' research and ability to communicate ideas. They can write essays about what they've learned. They can begin to identify what it takes to communicate effectively. Be sure to give all students an opportunity to be both exhibitor and listener.

Teaching Suggestions and Extension Ideas

1. Students need many opportunities to do research in order to become facile with the process. This does not mean that teachers have to assign four written reports over the year. The first time, have students go through the research and stop after they have recorded their notes on the webs. Grade the webs for organization and completeness. Share the best examples with the class.

A second research project could take the students through the same steps as the first, with the final product being a brief oral report. When students have taken all notes on their webs, model how to pick out and circle key words on the spokes. Allow students to use the webs as their notes for the oral report. The circled words will serve as triggers to help them remember the rest of the information. Grade both the webs (for organization and completeness) and the oral reports (for ability to communicate main ideas of their research.)

A third research project could take the students through all of the research and then require a visual which illustrates the main points learned. Grade both the webs and the visual (does it illustrate the main points?).

Finally, a fourth research project could require students to go through all the steps of research, write a rough draft of a report and produce a final copy. The webs, rough draft and final report would each be graded.

2. Use the **Topic-Subtopics Webs** as a way to review each unit of study that you complete in your curriculum. This will give students much needed practice distinguishing topics (general subject area) and subtopics (main ideas) from details.

3. If you are assigning projects along with written notes and/or a report, be sure to first require completion of the notes. Some students will avoid disciplining themselves to sit down, read and take notes. Instead, they will throw themselves into creating a game, a skit, a visual or art project, without first learning all about the topic. In the end, they will simply rush through the note taking to finish the requirements.

4. Send home the **Parent Report Notice** as soon as a student has missed a deadline. During these first exposures to reports and deadlines, it is important to hold the student accountable for *completing all* parts of the assignment. Invite students to suggest consequences for not meeting their deadlines.

Parent Report Notice

Your child's report on _____
                                                    (topic)

is due on _____.
                   (date)

In order to have students complete this report in a timely manner, without last-minute pressure, I have structured the assignment with several short-term deadlines. Your child has missed the deadline for handing in the following part of the assignment: _____

_____

_____

Please speak with him/her about his/her responsibility to complete this task immediately and to hand it in to me.

Failure to do so will result in the following: _____

_____

Thank you.

Sincerely, _____

Parent's Signature _____

Parent's Comments:

_____

_____

_____

_____

_____

_____

Topic - Subtopics Web

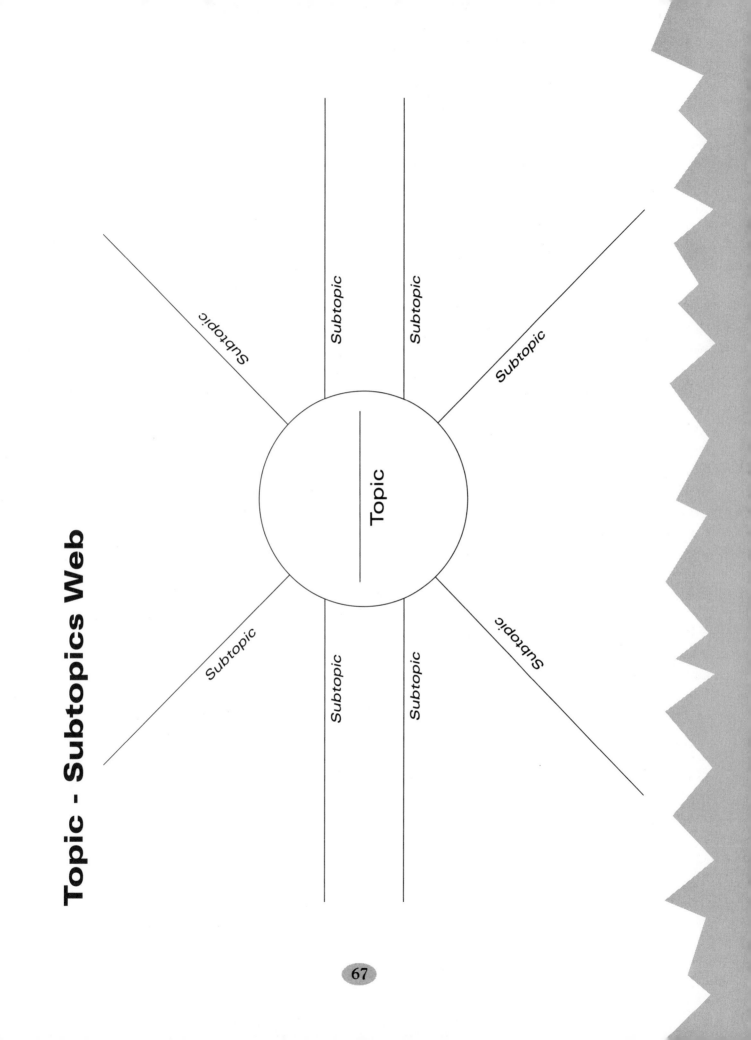

Topic

Subtopic

Subtopic

Subtopic

Subtopic

Subtopic

Subtopic

Subtopic

Subtopic

Web Method for Report Writing

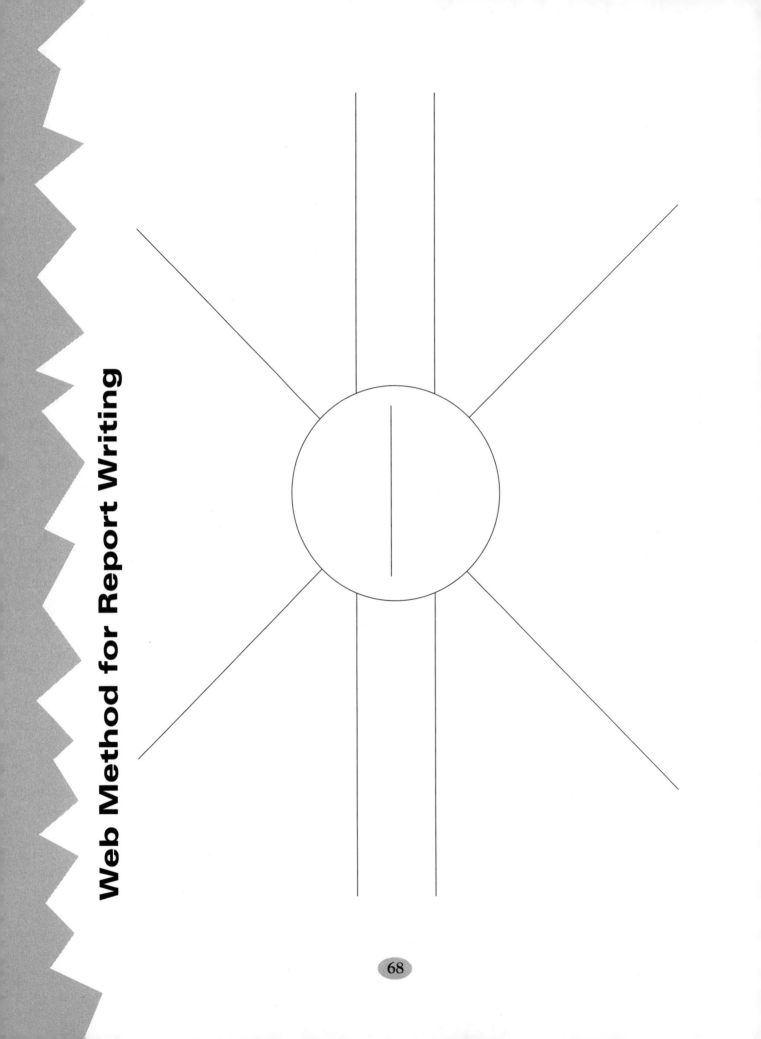

Chapter 7

Is Anybody Listening?
Improving Student Attention

Background

Helping students to develop listening skills is an often overlooked area of many educational programs. Yet students will spend more time listening in our classrooms than speaking, reading and writing combined. And as teachers, we often struggle just to get students to pay attention to us!

The ability to listen for detail, follow directions and evaluate what is heard is critical to the success of all students. Getting hired for a job depends on interviews which require these skills. Good listening will remain one of the most important skills a learner can develop for success in school and throughout the rest of his or her life.

In order to help students improve their listening skills, we must first understand that *hearing* what is said and *listening* to what is said are two very different things. Hearing is a mechanical and passive operation. We hear noises and sounds around us. When we listen, however, we make meaning out of those sounds; we follow along and think about what we are hearing. Listening involves a higher level of thinking. It takes concentration and the decision to pay attention to what's going on around us despite distractions.

We can help students to improve in this area by first having them recognize the skill and the effort it requires. Then, we can create a climate which rewards good listening and provides ample opportunities for students to process auditory input.

Advance Preparation

Have on hand copies of the following reproducibles:

✔ **Listening Facts** (*page 73*)
✔ **Noting What I've Learned** (*page 47*)

Strategies

Sum-It-Ups!

For students to absorb auditory information, we must allow them to *respond* at the end of a talk. It is helpful for visual learners to write a Sum-It-Up! in a section of their notebook set aside for this purpose. Give students three to four minutes to summarize their perception of the day's lesson. At first they may have difficulty with this activity; summarizing requires higher level thinking skills. You will need to model your own Sum-It-Ups! and ask several students to share theirs with the

class. In the beginning, students can simply list two or three new ideas that they learned that day. This activity will provide you with feedback about how well your students have perceived the main ideas of the lesson. The Sum-It-Ups! can be shared at the beginning of the next day's lesson as a review and will provide excellent summaries when studying for tests.

Listening Facts

After discussing a topic thoroughly in class, give students the **Listening Facts** reproducible and ask them to work in groups of three. The directions tell them to make statements about a topic, and then to draw a picture to illustrate all the statements. Be sure students understand that they do not have to draw well to use this strategy. Ask them how they think using this strategy helps them to learn and remember.

Group Think

After oral discussion, have students work in groups of three or four to allow for immediate review. Ask the group to react, synthesize and process the information by developing diagrams, semantic maps, lists, charts, mnemonic devices or any other tools which help make the information memorable. The immediate review helps process the information in long-term memory. The visuals created will serve as study tools for later.

Listening Situations

Set up listening situations that involve students in debates, oral reports, simulations and peer teaching. These activities actively engage the learners in meaningful ways. The listener can be trained to listen accurately for main ideas and to evaluate the speaker's point of view. Require all listeners to do something while listening: write a list of main ideas, complete a brief outline, list details to support a point of view, generate a list of questions which the speeches address. For homework, students can use their notes to summarize what they learned or support their own point of view. A modified Noting What I've Learned outline (see Chapter 4, *Better Note Taking*) can be used by students to record main ideas and a symbol or drawing that will help them remember the information.

Oral Warm-ups

To improve student attention when they are receiving directions, practice Oral Warm-ups regularly for a few months. As soon as class is supposed to begin, give a brief *oral* set of directions requiring students to complete a content-specific task within three or four minutes. For example, they can be asked to solve the first and last math problems on a certain page, write the description of the setting in a chapter of a novel they're reading or record all events between certain dates on a timeline in their Social Studies textbook.

Students write the answers in their notebook and record the date. They may not copy as you speak; this is a listening activity. They may not ask any questions, even of another student. You will not repeat the directions. Students will soon come to expect the routine and *choose* to listen more attentively.

Some teachers give an Oral Warm-up Quiz after two or three weeks where points are easily earned by having listened well. Students are simply asked to record the task given on a particular date.

Good Listening Behaviors

Generate a classroom list of "Good Listening Behaviors." Developed with students and posted in the front of the room as a daily reminder, the list may include statements such as: A good listener: looks directly at the speaker, is not doing other things, never talks when the speaker is talking, can repeat what he or she's heard, follows directions, thinks along with the speaker. Acknowledge and compliment students who use these desired behaviors.

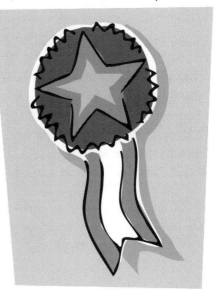

Good Listener Awards

Reward good listeners. Aside from positive verbal comments, give out Good Listener Awards to students who repeatedly demonstrate desired behaviors. In addition, each time you acknowledge students' positive listening behavior, give them a raffle ticket to write their name on and place in a box for a future drawing. Winners can choose from prizes such as stickers, baseball cards, pencils or book marks.

Teacher Talks

Teach students to listen for basic patterns in teacher talks by preparing several very organized presentations including: simple enumeration (e.g., "There are three things you need to know before you begin this experiment."), cause and effect, comparison and contrast, time sequence (e.g., first, second, next, then, finally), generalization and example (e.g., "Immigrants contributed much to our country. For example..."). Ask students to keep records of the types of patterns used by each of their teachers for one week. This exercise will raise their awareness that talks generally follow a pattern which makes what is being said easier to remember.

Listening Quiz

To teach students to pay attention to last minute directions, add a little twist to every quiz or test that you give. After handing out the papers, make a last minute change or give one additional direction to the students. (An example might be: Skip #11; choose only 1 essay; put your signature on the bottom of the page; answer only the odd numbers; when done with the test, fold it in half and place it on the left corner of your desk.) Make the directions brief and change something that is normally expected. Sometimes deduct points if students don't listen to directions. At other times, reward good listeners with bonus points. After a short while, students will become trained to listen for last minute directions.

Teaching Suggestions and Extension Ideas

1. Sometimes good listening brings its own obvious reward. If you choose to read passages related to your subject that are rich, fascinating, unusual or humorous, students will want to hear more. Begin each class for several days in a row with a descriptive oral reading, and watch students hurry to class to hear what's next.

2. As difficult as it is, train students to expect that you will give directions only once. Teachers who make this a goal report that after just a short time students chose to pay attention more closely the first time.

3. There are several ways to increase student listening to text material. First, read a passage from familiar material and omit important words. Ask students to fill them in. Next, read from the text and include incorrect words. Have students identify the errors and correct them. Finally, before reading a passage, tell students to listen for something specific, such as the reason something happened, the result of a particular incident, or the steps in a process.

4. Integrate listening activities into your daily lessons. Focus on a specific listening skill as you teach content. For instance, during a lesson on events leading up to the Civil War, you might want to focus on the listening skill of sequencing.

Listening Facts

Topic

Step 1: Student A makes 1 statement about the topic.

Step 2: Student B repeats the statement and adds 1 fact.

Step 3: Student C repeats both statements and adds 1 fact.

Step 4: Draw a picture which illustrates all 3 statements.

C h a p t e r   8

Time Management

Getting It All Done

Background

Frequently I encounter students who wait until the very last minute to begin work on a long-term assignment or book report. Their parents describe them as "lazy" and express frustration with trying to help them complete assignments in a timely fashion. Their teachers receive the products of their last-minute rush and wonder how much they learned in this scramble to finish at the eleventh hour. My experience with those students tells me that they are simply overwhelmed and do not know where to begin.

Although some students will continue to work in this fashion even as adults, it is important that we offer training to *all* of our students about how to break down assignments into smaller steps to be accomplished over time. Many students would choose to work with a plan if they realized that doing so meant less stress for them in school, as well as at home. To help students to use schedules, we must frequently talk about how long it actually takes to complete a particular task and we must model

75

how to break long-term assignments down into small steps. Then, we must hold students accountable for accomplishing each short-term goal by a certain deadline. (See Chapter 6, *Better Report Writing*, for more strategies related to time management and report writing.)

Advance Preparation

Prepare copies of the following reproducibles:

✔ **My Daily Planner** (*page 78*)
✔ **Project Planner** (*page 79*)
✔ **Monthly Calendar** (*page 80*).

Strategies

My Daily Planner

Show students how to use **My Daily Planner** on those days which are particularly busy or overwhelming for them. By listing all "must-dos" as well as all "want-to-dos," students learn the important skill of setting priorities. Teach students to list such things as homework, studying for a test, chores, lessons, reading and practicing an instrument on their planner. Teach them to check off each item as it is completed so they gain a feeling of accomplishment. Finally, show them how to carry an unaccomplished task to the next day's Planner.

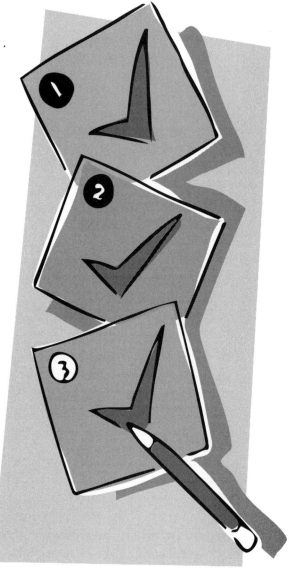

Project Planner

A **Project Planner** should be used when you give a project or assignment that is due in approximately one week. After modeling how to break down such assignments a few times for the class, let students work in pairs to plan a schedule for their next project. They can learn from one another even if the project is to be done individually.

One of the advantages of the Project Planner is that the seven-day plan can begin on any day of the week and it will still include two weekend days that are broken down into four parts. Looking at this visual plan, students can choose to use a portion of the weekend to catch up from their busy weekdays. By writing out a goal for each day, they can schedule more work on less busy days so they continue to move towards completion of their projects.

Monthly Calendar

The **Monthly Calendar** is helpful when assigning long-term reports or projects. Weekly goals are set, instead of the daily goals of the Project Planner. Students can record how many chapters they need to read each week for a book report, when they will visit the library, how many times they will read and take notes and when they will write their rough drafts and final copies. Reaching weekly goals helps students feel that they are in control of their work. If they do not accomplish their goals by the end of the week, students have time to adjust and work harder over the weekend and during the following week, before too many things pile up.

Making Time Predictions

Some students take forever to do their homework, because they lack the discipline to sit in one place and focus their attention. To help students build these skills, teach them to approximate how long an assignment will take. For example, if one math problem takes 20 seconds to finish, then 30 problems should take approximately 10 minutes. Make predictions on how long students should take to complete classwork assignments. Explain to students that there will always be a range of time based on different work styles. As students copy their homework onto the **Homework Log** (see Chapter 1, *Organizational Skills*) or on an assignment pad, also have them write an estimate of how long the work should take. At first you will have to help them guess by giving your own expectations of the assignment. Take a minute the following day to see how long homework actually took. Some students would benefit from using a timer to help them focus on the task.

Parents will welcome any ideas for getting children to increase concentration during homework time. Include a note about making predictions about how long an assignment should take in your newsletter home. (See Chapter 10, *The Parent Connection*, for more information on newsletters and reaching parents.)

Teaching Suggestions and Extensions Ideas

1. Make **Project Planners** part of every project you give. This planning stage is a good place for parents to be included in the educational process. They can be instructed to sit with their child to help develop workable schedules. Parents should not do the report with their child. Rather, they should help to see that the plan is adhered to.

My Daily Planner
Things To Do Today!

Date: _____

I MUST Do: *

Completed

1. _____ ☐
2. _____ ☐
3. _____ ☐
4. _____ ☐
5. _____ ☐
6. _____ ☐
7. _____ ☐
8. _____ ☐

I WANT To Do:

1. _____ ☐
2. _____ ☐
3. _____ ☐
4. _____ ☐
5. _____ ☐

*List things such as homework, studying for a test, chores, lessons, reading, practicing the piano.

Project Planner

Assignment: _____ Due Date: _____

	Day 1	Day 2	Day 3	Day 4	Day 5	Day 6	Day 7
Morning							
Early Afternoon							
Late Afternoon							
Evening							

79

Monthly Calendar

Month _____ Year _____

SUNDAY	MONDAY	TUESDAY	WEDNESDAY	THURSDAY	FRIDAY	SATURDAY	WEEKLY GOALS*

*What I want to have accomplished by the end of this week.

80

Chapter 9

Learning Through Visualization

Picturing It In Your Mind

Background

Most students are visual learners and would benefit from teaching methods which include creating visual representations of information. We must model and walk them through strategies which teach them to visualize so they learn to do this on their own.

When we hold pictures in our mind's eye, we are able to remember a great deal of information. Looking over photos taken on a family trip, we are flooded with memories and details about the experience. We can show students how that same ability to remember can be cultivated using visualizing strategies during study time. Such strategies not only match the learning style of most of our students, but also guarantee greater recall of detail. The brain recalls more when it processes information and ideas through words *and* through pictures.

Advance Preparation

Prepare copies of:

✔ **Filming the Idea** (*page 85*)

81

Strategies

Graphic Organizers

Graphic organizers are semantic maps (word maps) which offer a visual representation of ideas. When students organize and design these maps, they apply important analytical skills as they think about how ideas are interrelated. Abstract information is put into concrete and visual form which can be "pictured in one's mind" and more readily retrieved later.

Examples of ways to organize information visually are shown below.

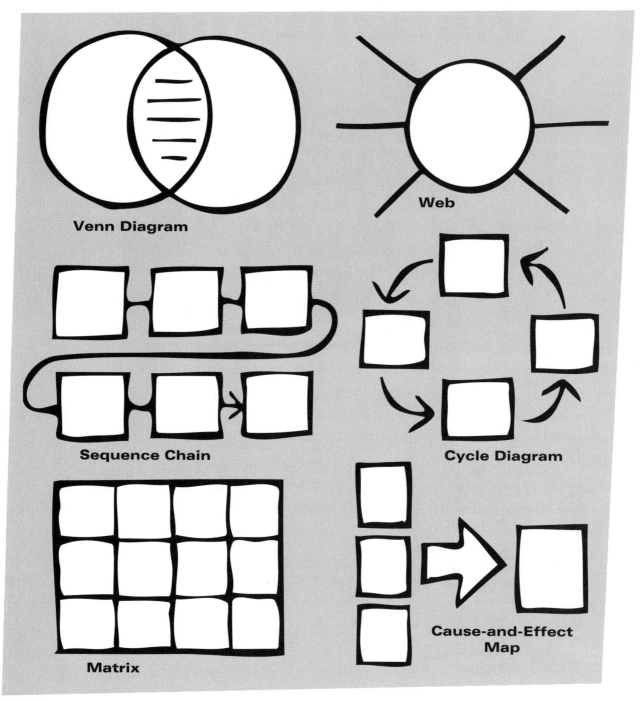

Venn Diagram

Web

Sequence Chain

Cycle Diagram

Matrix

Cause-and-Effect Map

Filming The Idea

Using the **Filming the Idea** reproducible, students draw pictures to help them remember information. For example, by drawing two significant events from the beginning, the middle and the end of any story or chapter, students can use this strategy to learn to summarize. The pictures they create can be used for an oral book report, a summary of the steps in a science experiment or a review of a period in history. Suggest that students staple two or more Filming the Idea pages together if they want to draw additional pictures.

Creating Visual Symbols

After completion of a unit of study, have students form groups and let each group choose a subtopic to review. Ask group members decide on five to ten *significant* concepts such as ideas, causes, results, events, and people, which are related to their subtopic and choose symbols which could represent each one. For homework ask each member of the group to draw or trace one or two symbols on flashcards.

The following day, have each group present a brief oral review of their information using their flashcards. Then pass each set of flashcards around to the different groups. Ask students to explain the significance of each symbol and how it relates to the main topic of study. Label and store the flashcards for use in future review.

Student-Made Books

Student-Made Books can be created for any unit of study or piece of literature. Designed by students, they are simplified and illustrated versions of the material studied. The books can be used to teach younger or less able students material from texts which are often above their reading levels. They can be used as an advance organizer to introduce students to a new unit of study. The actual writing of the material forces the learner to analyze the information and evaluate what is most significant about the topic. The drawings help the learner synthesize the information in a holistic and visual way, making the retrieval of information easier.

Use plain paper to create the books. Draw several lines on the bottom half of the page for the writing. Then simply bind several pieces of the paper together by stapling along the side or top and covering the staples with colored cloth tape.

Mind Over Matter

Over the years, most teachers have gathered posters, models and other materials to supplement their texts. After exhibiting and describing one of these visuals to the class, have your students study it silently for a couple of minutes. Then ask them to close their eyes and think about the visual for one or two minutes. Put the visual out of sight. When they open their eyes, ask students to draw what they remember or to write what they remember in a paragraph.

Teaching Suggestions and Extension Ideas

1. Try to include some type of graphic organizer in each lesson. When using any semantic map, be sure to model its use and explain how it helps to organize the information, so future retrieval is easier. Use webs to introduce a new lesson (activating prior knowledge or making new connections) and summarize a completed unit. At the end of a Social Studies lesson, for example, pair students off to design sequence charts to illustrate the events leading up to an important event (such as the American Revolution or the Civil War); in a Science class they can use a sequence chart to show the steps they took in doing an experiment. After students have read several pages or chapters assigned for English class, ask them to design a flow chart to show plot development or the development of a particular character, a Venn diagram to compare their lives to that of the main character's or a web which states a theme of a story (subtopic) and shows examples from the story (details).

2. For homework, have students use a graphic organizer to organize the information they learned in one class that day. Have students work in groups the next day to share their organizers and evaluate their usefulness. You can provide blank organizers, but be sure to teach students how to make them on their own, as well. Provide frequent opportunities for your students to choose which organizer to use in order to show how certain information is related.

3. You can increase your students' ability to visualize if you frequently ask them to close their eyes and think along with you as you give them a description of something. For example, in a Science class, have students close their eyes while you describe the four food groups. Then have them open their eyes and draw foods which fall into each category.

4. Explain to students that if they use visualizing techniques while they study, they will remember a great deal of detail. Tell them to finish each reading assignment by closing their eyes and picturing what they just read. When we review information immediately after learning it for the first time, we are able to remember a great deal more of the details later on.

5. When having students create visual symbols, you will have to check each group's list of significant ideas. You may need to add concepts that they have overlooked or eliminate ideas which are really too minor. Save the best flashcards from each class to make a master set you can duplicate.

6. Students working on projects or performing experiments will benefit from visualizing the steps they need to follow in order to complete the assignment. Have them close their eyes and listen as you describe the steps. When they open their eyes, pair them off and ask them to repeat the correct order of the steps to one another. Then, have them list the steps on a sequence chain.

Filming
The
Idea

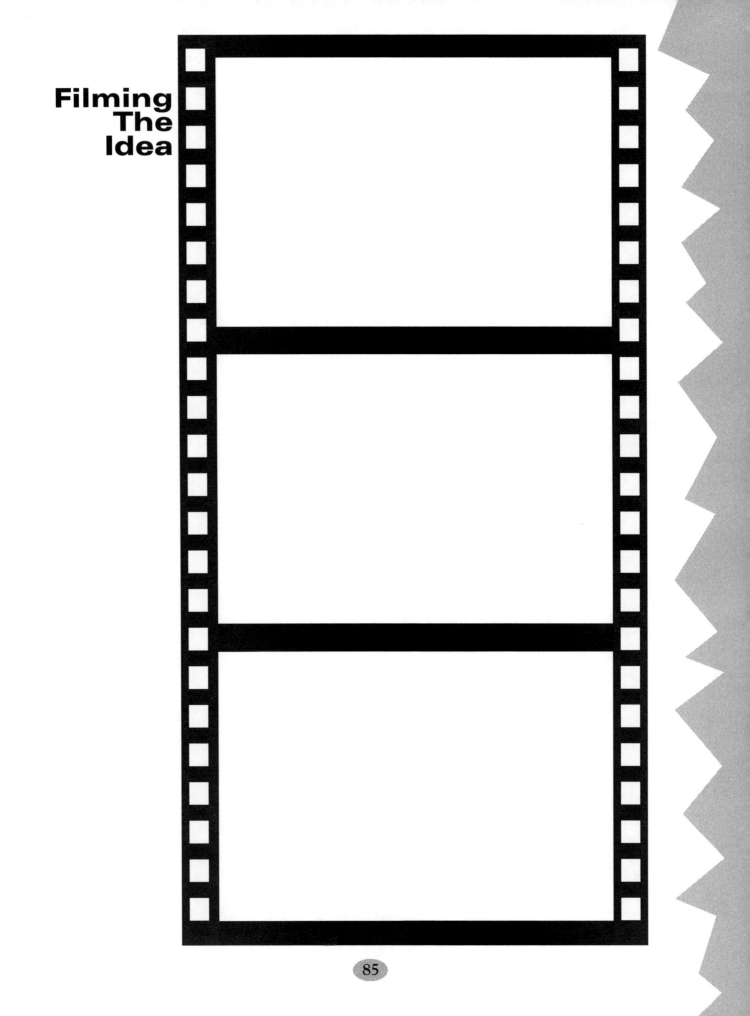

Chapter 10

The Parent Connection

Getting Help From Home

Background

Recent studies indicate that the most successful students are those whose parents are involved with their education. As teachers we need to educate parents about how they should be involved and what they can do at home to foster their children's learning. Many parents would like to encourage their children but have no idea how to go about it.

Advance Preparation

You may want to have on hand copies of the following reproducibles:

✔ **Parent Newsletter** (*page 89*)
✔ **ParenTips** (*page 90*)

Strategies

Parent Newsletter

One of the best ways to stay in touch with parents and communicate your ideas to them is to send a newsletter home. Although this may seem time-consuming, the benefits make it worth writing: parents cannot complain that they don't know what is going on in the classroom or aren't aware of major projects and deadlines. Some teachers send a weekly letter informing parents of topics studied, problems encountered, ways to help their child practice a particular skill, upcoming assignments and so on. Others send a monthly newsletter which brings the parents up-to-date. In either case, it is a good idea to include a place for parents to sign and write any comments they may have. You may want to write your own letter, or you can use the **Parent Newsletter**.

Student Interviews

In an effort to involve the whole community in the educational process, have students engage in interviews with their parents, relatives, teachers and administrators to determine what their best study strategies were when they went to school. Tell students to record the strategies and put together a booklet of the best ideas. They also can draw and display posters to illustrate some of the strategies.

Parent Day

Parents can be invited to visit the class to share their thoughts about their own education and the skills and courses they needed in order to prepare for their occupations. This will provide students with practical reasons to work at their studies.

ParenTips

Periodically, send parents a simple list of ideas that they can use at home to improve learning. These lists, such as **ParenTips**, can include ideas to encourage reading and writing, foster better math skills, organize materials for homework and study, or design a "study office."

Parent Education Workshops

Parent workshops provide an excellent opportunity to train parents to support what is going on in school. Often, P.T.A. groups will provide such a forum and teachers will present strategies for parents to use at home with their children. Unfortunately, too few parents attend the large group meetings. If it is possible for you to schedule your own parent session, attendance will probably be greater. The web on the next page shows how I organize such a workshop. Some teachers have run Parent-Child Workshops with great success. The child comes with his or her parent and together they learn how to approach a textbook assignment or study for a test. The parents learn from the teacher just how involved they should be in the child's studying. The parent/child team learns to work together toward the goal having the child become more skilled at studying on his or her own.

Homework Helpers

Parents can provide support to teachers by organizing an after-school Homework Helpers Program. Staffed by parent volunteers, the program offers students a place to work on homework and receive assistance. Parents can be polled to find out who has strength in a particular subject area. Volunteers can be coached by a teacher/administrator team in order to learn general strategies for helping students get organized and have greater success in school. Refreshments can be provided.

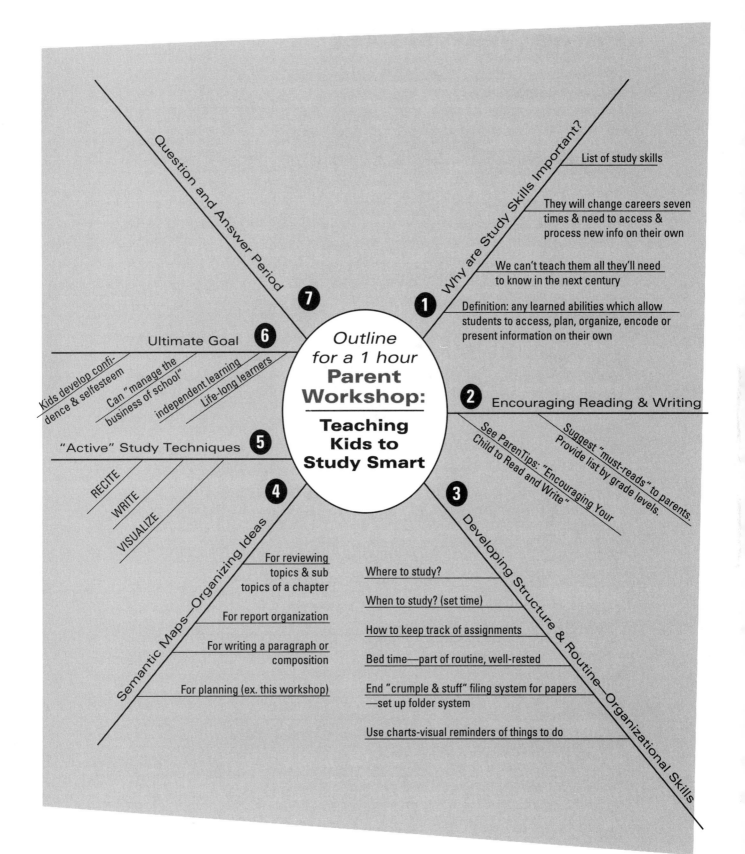

Question and Answer Period

Why are Study Skills Important?

List of study skills

They will change careers seven times & need to access & process new info on their own

We can't teach them all they'll need to know in the next century

Definition: any learned abilities which allow students to access, plan, organize, encode or present information on their own

Ultimate Goal

Kids develop confidence & selfesteem

Can "manage the business of school"

independent learning

Life-long learners

Outline for a 1 hour Parent Workshop:

Teaching Kids to Study Smart

Encouraging Reading & Writing

Suggest "must-reads" to parents.
Provide list by grade levels.

See ParenTips: "Encouraging Your Child to Read and Write"

"Active" Study Techniques

RECITE

WRITE

VISUALIZE

Semantic Maps—Organizing Ideas

For reviewing topics & sub topics of a chapter

For report organization

For writing a paragraph or composition

For planning (ex. this workshop)

Developing Structure & Routine—Organizational Skills

Where to study?

When to study? (set time)

How to keep track of assignments

Bed time—part of routine, well-rested

End "crumple & stuff" filing system for papers —set up folder system

Use charts-visual reminders of things to do

1 2 3 4 5 6 7

Parent Newsletter

Date: _____

Teacher: _____

This week/month we studied the following:

Ask your child to tell you about...

Upcoming tests and/or projects include...

For your information, I would like you to know...

Sincerely, _____

Parent's signature and comment: _____

_____

_____

_____

_____

_____

_____

ParenTips
Encouraging Your Child To Read and Write

✔ Read to your child daily.

✔ Read the comics together.

✔ Let your child read the television or movie schedule aloud to you.

✔ Encourage your child to look up telephone numbers in the phone book.

✔ Give the gift of a book or magazine subscription on a topic of special interest to your reluctant reader.

✔ Ask your child to read the menu at a restaurant to you.

✔ Ask your child to read signs wherever you go.

✔ Have your child read aloud the writing on cereal boxes, juice containers and so on, as you prepare breakfast.

✔ Record a favorite story or magazine article so that your child can listen to the words while reading.

✔ Leave funny little notes (jokes, friendly reminders, thank-yous) around the house— on a blackboard, in a lunch box, on the bathroom mirror, on the refrigerator door.

✔ Have your child trace pictures from the comics and write his or her own captions.

✔ Have your child write the weekly grocery list as you look through the cabinets and dictate.

✔ Provide letter stamps or letter stencils for creating fun projects such as birthday invitations, valentine cards, or posters for your child's bedroom door or school locker.

✔ Use any excuse to have your child create a poster or sign for your family (Welcome Home! Get Well Soon! The Party's Here! Great Job, Bobby! Congratulations, Mom!).

✔ Encourage your child to write a fan letter to a favorite sports, television or music personality.

✔ Encourage your child to send away for, or obtain from your library, *Free Stuff For Kids* (Meadowbrook Press, Deephaven, MN 55391).

✔ Have your child tell you a story while you write it down. Then reverse things: you dictate a short story as your child writes. Ignore spelling. Your goal here is to encourage the desire to write, not to teach spelling. "Creative" spelling is just fine if your child can read it back to you.

✔ Have your child plan a menu for a special occasion. Let him or her look through recipe books for a new recipe and copy it on a recipe card. Help him or her prepare the recipe and hand out a photocopy of the recipe card to all the dinner guests.

✔ Create a Family Foto Center on a bulletin board. Put up favorite photos, and have your child write funny comments under each one. Change the photos and comments periodically and encourage your child to read them to visitors.

✔ Write and illustrate books together. Have your child draw several pictures about one topic (such as a recent trip, winter activities, a day at school). Have him or her write or dictate to you a sentence about each picture. Bind the pages together using yarn or staples covered with vinyl tape.

✔ Create a family newsletter to send to relatives. Encourage your kids to interview a relative, write an article about some bit of family news, describe a family tradition, include a favorite family recipe or write a special poem for each other. Your older child may want to type or use the computer to publish the newsletter. Otherwise, you can simply photocopy the children's writing.

Index of Strategies

Boldface type indicates a reproducible.

Bibliography

Bragstad, Bernice J. and Sharyn M. Stumpf. *A Guidebook for Teaching: Study Skills and Motivation*. Newton, Massachusetts: Allyn and Bacon, Inc., 1987.

Burkel, Candace Regan and David Marshak. *Study Skills Program: Level 1*. Reston, Virginia: The National Association of Elementary School Principals and the National Association of Seconday School Principals, 1980.

Dansereau, Donald. "Dyadic Text Learning Strategy." *Journal of Reading*. April 1987.

Devine, Thomas G. *Teaching Study Skills: A Guide for Teachers*. Old Tappan, New Jersey: Allyn and Bacon, Inc., 1986.

Dodge, Judy. "Study Smart: Innovative Ways to Foster Independent Learning in Every Student." New York: *Instructor Magazine*, 1993

Dodge, Judy, Diane Abrams, Rita Bartenback, Barbara Campassano, and Luise M. Lutz. *Study Survival Guide: The Path to School Success*. New York, 1993.

Kesselman-Turkel, Judi and Franklynn Peterson. *Note-Taking Made Easy*. Chicago, Illinois: Contemporary Books, Inc., 1982

Pauk, Walter. *How to Study in College*. Boston: Houghton Mifflin, 1984.

Vacca, Jo Anne L., Richard T. Vacca and and Mary K. Gove. *Reading and Learning to Read*. Boston: Little, Brown and Company, 1987.

Walsh, Frank. *The Regis Study Skills Guide*. Worcester, Massachusetts: The Hefferman Press, 1980.

Weinstein, Claire E., Ernest T. Goetz and Patricia Alexander. *Learning and Study Strategies: Issues in Assessment, Instruction, and Evaluation*. San Diego, California: Academic Press, 1988.